MAKING
NEEDLEWORK ACCESSORIES

MAKING

NEEDLEWORK

ACCESSORIES

EMBROIDERED WITH BEADS

CAROL ANDREWS

RUTH
BEAN

First published 2004 in the United Kingdom by
Ruth Bean *Publishers*
Victoria Farmhouse, Carlton, Bedford MK43 7LP

ISBN 0 903585 33 2
A catalogue record for this book is available from the
British Library.

Bead embroidery advisor Vera Gray
Design Ted Harrison
Photography Mark Scudder, Photographic Dept,
    Cambridge University Library
Photo styling Victoria Simons
Electronic page make-up Norman Tilley Graphics,
    Northampton
Printed in Hong Kong by CTPS

Cover
Front: Selection of needlework accessories.
Back: Pin cushion hat from p.30.

Frontispiece
Victorian style bodkin holder, p.19.

Contents

List of plates

Introduction

Some years ago, inspired by a bead embroidered Victorian needle book found at a local textiles auction, I resolved to try making something similar myself. I drew a pattern and selected the smallest seed beads generally available though amazingly these were still larger than the beads on the antique version!

The resulting needle book was very satisfying to make, and the project fired the interest of my students, with whom it remains a firm favourite. It also inspired us to seek out other projects, adapting the embroidery outline and developing a whole set of co-ordinated accessories in the same Victorian style, as you will see in Chapter 1.

The projects will appeal particularly to embroiderers who like working on small-scale projects, especially those who admire old beaded needlework accessories. Work with magnification if you need it, but always choose a type that leaves both hands free.

As many have discovered, this is not an expensive hobby. With a quarter metre of silk and a few packets of beads and threads you can make several very appealing colour co-ordinated accessories.

There is much interest in miniature items nowadays and the patterns in this book can easily be adapted to other applications including dolls house furnishings. Imagine the floral border on p.29 embroidered on dolls house curtains, for example.

You can adapt the patterns for your own purposes, and even make a personal fashion statement. Some of the designs look wonderful on clothing, from denim outfits to bridal wear. You may need to enlarge the embroidery outline and use larger beads and threads. Just remember that the embroidery must be worked on a hoop.

Happy stitching!

Acknowledgements

Besides the inspiration received for this book from many unknown Victorian needlewomen I am also glad to acknowledge the indispensable and more recent contribution of those involved in its publication.

My thanks go first to my embroidery and upholstery students. They responded enthusiastically to a new challenge and helped develop the impressive results, as illustrated in the fine work of June Batchelor, Coral Harrison, Pam Hancock, Helen Payne, and Lynette Williams. Lynette also developed the section on beaded picot edgings.

I am grateful to Vera Gray for valuable technical advice; to Ray Coggle, silversmith, for designing and supplying many beautiful needlework tools to complete the accessories; to Mark Scudder again for his fine photography; and to Victoria Simons for her inspired styling.

I would also like to acknowledge with special gratitude the invaluable contribution of my publishers, Ruth and Nigel Bean, and their high standards. This book has reached publication only due to their patience and skills.

How to use the book

The projects are grouped by subjects or style. The Victorian and Beaded lotus projects follow particular design styles, while different floral motifs can be found in From the garden. The final group of projects features Gifts and keepsakes. The Techniques section provides the supporting instructions to work and make up the projects.

Projects are not presented in order of difficulty, but a simple Starter project and Practice pieces are provided. To gain further experience on techniques, work a project such as the Pin cushion with floral border or the Victorian needle book before tackling the most advanced designs such as the Beaded lotus or Pin basket projects.

Before starting a project you should read carefully the sections *Tools and materials* and *Preparing to embroider.*

- Prepare the tools and materials you will need. Measurements are given in both millimetres and inches.
- An embroidery hoop is essential: both bead embroidery and couching stitches require the needle to pass vertically up and down through a stretched fabric, which can only be achieved on a hoop.
- Choose a silk with a smooth surface: beads won't sit well on a slubby fabric. The silk is lined before use, so subsequent references to the silk fabric mean the lined silk.
- When selecting beads use the coloured illustrations as a guide. You may prefer to select other colour combinations, perhaps using materials you already hold, but make sure that the beads match the sizes specified in the project.
- Bead sizes follow the international code, e.g. 11°. The higher the number the smaller the bead. Metallic purl (bullion or gimp), though thread-like, is a coil and is stitched like a bead.
- Match the beading thread to the colour of the beads as this will enhance the appearance of your embroidery.

- Stitches used are listed at the start of each project. In the Embroidery notes, stitches shown initially in **bold** type are explained within the project, and those in ***bold italics*** in the Techniques section, where all the stitches are listed in its Table of contents, p.63. Plain *italics* refer to project titles or chapters in the Techniques section throughout. Flag the relevant pages before starting.
- Your work will look best if you can keep the beads firmly upright. So it is important to match the length of stitch to the bead hole.
- Try practising beading stitches on a spare piece of calico or fine cotton stretched in a hoop, as for the *Practice pieces*, before beading on silk.
- *Embroidery notes* for a project are set out in the order of working. As you progress, check each stage against the bullet points listed.
- A beading diagram is given for each project and working diagrams are included throughout to explain specific steps in beading, couching and making up.
- Where plates and diagrams are shown actual size this is stated in the caption.
- Left-handed embroiderers may find it helpful to view the diagrams in a mirror.
- *Making up*, or construction, may be new territory for some embroiderers but by following the instructions closely you should be able to achieve really satisfying results, as can be seen from the finished items.

Projects

You will need

Denim fabric, marked with the outlines of the purse pattern parts.

Size 9° beads, fine embroidery needles and Nymo or polyester thread; a light-coloured pencil to mark the positions of the flowers; DMC size 5 red *coton perlé* thread for the twisted cord strap.

Beading notes

You can bead these simple flowers in the hand or work on a hoop frame, but do this before the fabric is made up.

Mark the embroidery outline, Fig 1. Start with the left flower, see *Starting and fastening off*. Other techniques used, shown in **bold italics**, are also given in the Techniques section. ***Double stitch*** a single bead for the flower centre. Next, bead the ring of eight 'petals', Figs 2 and 3. Work the second and third flower in the same way. Make the ***twisted cord*** for the strap and make up the purse to match the illustration.

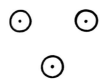

1. Embroidery outline
Mark the dots and circles on the right side of the fabric with the pencil: the top two horizontally, 18 mm (¾ in) apart along the same thread line, and the third 12 mm (½ in) below.

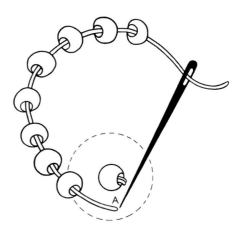

2. Threading the ring of beads
Double-stitch the centre bead. Bring up the needle at A inside the pattern marking, shown here by a broken circle. The distance between A and the centre bead should be half a bead width.

Thread enough beads to complete a circle within the pattern marking and insert the needle close to A, but do not pull it through the fabric yet. To finalise the number required, push the beads down to the base of the thread, and lay them just inside the pattern marking. You can adjust the number of beads at this stage if necessary. Take the needle through and gently pull the thread taut.

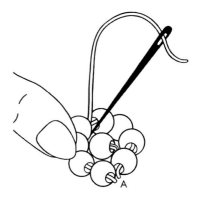

3. Securing the ring of beads
Hold the ring temporarily with your thumb so the beads fit snugly round the centre bead.

Bring up the needle outside the ring between two beads at a point opposite A. To secure the circle work a *couching stitch* over the beading thread. Make two further couching stitches round the ring, each between a pair of beads.

Beaded flowers on denim

Making this trio of brightly-beaded flowers on a child's denim purse will introduce you to some of the skills needed for embroidery with beads. The flowers will also look good on items of denim clothing, including jeans, pockets and collars.

Green, yellow and red opaque seed beads on indigo denim were used for this girl's purse. The 90 cm (3 ft) twisted cord strap was made with five strands of DMC size 5 red *coton perlé* thread, 2.5 m (8 ft) long. Actual size.

1 *Victorian style*

Needle book
Scissors case
Bodkin and needle holder
Thimble slipper

Needle book
Designed and worked by the author

This is the simpler of the needle book patterns. It introduces basic techniques and has been worked by many beginners. The embroidery and edging were inspired by a Victorian needle book in a local antiques auction.
See Plates 9 and 10 for practice pieces.

You will need
Embroidery hoop 18 cm (7 in), tracing paper and HB pencil, tissue paper and white dressmaker's carbon paper. Embroidery needles sizes 8 and 12 and short beading needles size 12.
Fabric. Fine plain Burgundy Indian silk, minimum 25 cm (10 in) square. Same amount of fine iron-on interlining, e.g. vilene softline or pellon.
Threads. Single strand of gold metallic cord, gold 100% viscose thread; grey Nymo* beading thread gauge D, or polyester thread.
Beads. Seed beads: size 11°, pearl pink; size 15° pearl ivory, gun-metal grey and mat gold.
Construction. See *Making up – needle books.*
* Nymo beading threads are sold in the UK without reference numbers. They must be conditioned before use by thorough stretching, to make them pliable and maintain an even tension.

Stitches
Beading 6- to 8-petal flowers, couching metallic thread, threading and couching beads, single-stitching a bead.

All stitches and techniques are shown in the Embroidery notes in **bold italics** and, together with *Starting and fastening off threads* and directions for *Making up* will be found in the Techniques section, or on specified pages and Figures. You may need to refer to them while working the project.

Victorian style needle book
Embroidered with seed beads, sizes 11° and 15°, and metallic cord on fine Burgundy Indian silk.
 Stems are in gold metallic cord couched with gold viscose thread.
 Flower centres are pearl pink beads 11°; *petals* in pearl ivory 15°; *leaves* and *buds* in gun-metal grey 15°; *bud tips* in mat gold 15°. The beaded *picot edging* is in gun-metal grey and pearl ivory 15°. Actual size.

Embroidery notes

Trace the embroidery outline, Fig 1 (*on p.16*), and transfer it and the pattern parts on to the silk, following the procedure on p.67. This includes mounting the silk on to the hoop, ready for embroidery.

FRONT

Work in the following stages:

- bead the flowers lying directly across a stem
- **couch** the main stem, then the shorter stems
- work the remaining flowers
- **thread and couch** the leaves and buds

Flowers and stems

1. Follow Fig 2 and bead the three flowers marked *, p.82. **Double-stitch** a pearl pink bead 11° for the centre. **Back-stitch** six or seven pearl ivory beads 15° for the petals (as used here) or try the **quicker method**, p.81.
2. For the main stem start at the top. **Couch** a single thickness of metallic cord with gold viscose along the stem line as shown, **plunging** the cord and thread behind the flowers already beaded, and bringing them up again just in front, see Figs 1, 3 and 4 in *Couching threads*.
3. Work the remaining stems. It is important to tidy the ends of metallic cord on the back of the fabric to avoid a tangle, see Fig 6 in *Couching threads*.
4. Bead the remaining flowers.

Leaves

5. Leaves are shown on the embroidery outline as short curved lines. **Thread and couch** a line of 2 or 3 gun-metal grey beads, 15°.

Buds

6. Buds are shown as narrow ovals on the embroidery outline. Use the same method as for leaves, adding a mat gold bead, 15°, at the tip.

BACK AND SPINE

The position of these pattern parts should already have been outlined on the silk.

7. Remove the embroidery from the hoop, but don't cut out any pattern parts yet. For construction see *Making up*, and for the **picot edging** see *Edgings*.

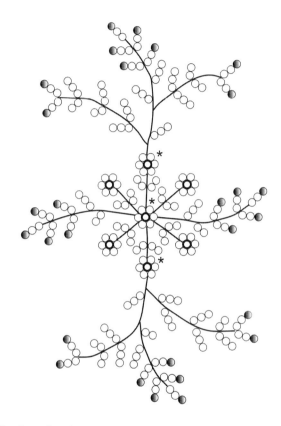

2. Guide to beading

Key

Lines – metallic cord
   curved and straight lines – stems: single strand gold metallic cord couched with viscose thread.
Circles – seed beads, sizes 11° and 15°
   heavier circles – centres of flowers: pearl pink, 11°.
   fine circles – ring of flower petals, leaves and buds, picot edging: pearl ivory, gun-metal grey 15°.
   solid circles – tips of buds: mat gold, 15°.
Starting from the top first embroider the three flowers marked *, p.82. Then, also from the top, *couch* the main stem, *plunging* the cord and thread behind the flowers already worked and bringing them up again just in front, p.86.
   Couch the remaining stems. Bead the remaining flowers. *Thread and couch* the lines of beads for the leaves, then the buds, adding a mat gold bead, 15° at the tip.

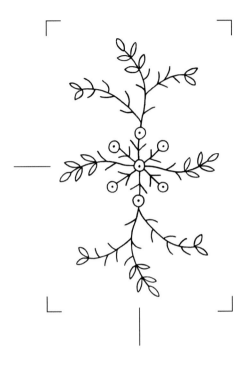

◄ **1. Embroidery outline for needle book**
Solid lines show stems, circles indicate flowers. The short curved offshoots indicate leaves, and oval shapes the buds.

Carefully trace the outline, the locating lines and corner marks, see *Preparing to embroider*. Actual size.

1. Embroidery outline for scissors case ►
Solid lines show stems, circles indicate flowers. The short curved offshoots indicate leaves, and oval shapes the buds.

Carefully trace the outline, the locating lines and corner marks, see *Preparing to embroider*. Actual size.

Scissors case

Embroidered with seed beads size 15°, and silver metallic embroidery floss, on the mat side of plain purple satin.

Stems in silver metallic floss couched with silver viscose thread.

Flower centres in pink pearl beads; *petals* in white pearl.

Leaves and *buds* in translucent blue pink-lined beads; *bud tips* in translucent silver-lined beads. The case is edged with twisted cord in purple silk thread. Actual size.

Scissors case

A traditional pattern adapted and embroidered by Coral Harrison.
   See Plates 9 and 10 for practice pieces.

You will need

Embroidery hoop 18 cm (7 in), tracing paper and HB pencil, tissue paper and white dressmaker's carbon paper. Embroidery needles sizes 8 and 12 and short beading needles size 12.

Fabric. Fine plain purple satin, minimum 25 cm (10 in) square. Same amount of fine iron-on interlining, e.g. vilene softline or pellon.

Threads. Stranded silver metallic embroidery floss, silver 100% viscose thread; grey Nymo* beading thread gauge D, or polyester thread; purple embroidery silk for twisted cord.

Beads. Seed beads: all size 15°, pearl pink, pearl white, translucent blue pink-lined, translucent silver-lined.

Construction. See *Making up – scissors case.*

* Nymo beading threads are sold in the UK without reference numbers. They must be conditioned before use by thorough stretching, to make them pliable and maintain an even tension.

Stitches

Beading 6- to 8-petal flowers, couching metallic thread, threading and couching beads, single-stitching a bead.

All stitches and techniques are shown in the Embroidery notes in **bold italics** and, together with *Starting and fastening off threads* and directions for *Making up* will be found in the Techniques section, or on specified pages and Figures. You may need to refer to them while working the project.

Embroidery notes

Trace the embroidery outline, Fig 1, and transfer it and the pattern parts on to the silk, following the procedure on p.67. This includes mounting the silk on to the hoop, ready for embroidery.

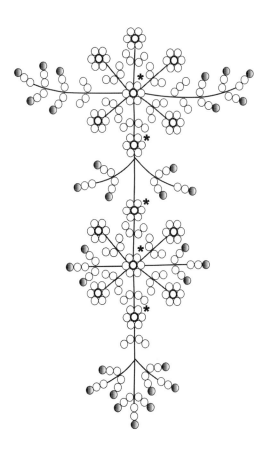

2. Guide to beading for scissors case

Key

Lines – stranded metallic embroidery floss

   curved and straight lines – stems: horizontal stems are two
   strand, and the rest single strand silver metallic floss
   couched with viscose thread.

Circles – seed beads, all size 15°

   heavier circles – centre of flowers: pearl pink.

   fine circles – ring of flower petals, leaves and buds: pearl
   white and translucent blue pink-lined.

   solid circles – tips of buds: translucent silver-lined.

Starting from the top first embroider the five flowers
marked *, p.82. Then, also from the top, *couch* the main stem,
plunging the cord and thread behind the flowers already
worked and bringing them up again just in front, p.86. *Couch*
the remaining stems. Bead the remaining flowers. *Thread and
couch* the lines of beads for the leaves, then the buds, adding
the translucent silver-lined bead at the tip.

Work in the following stages:

• bead the five flowers lying directly across a stem
• **couch** the main stem, then the shorter stems
• work the remaining flowers,
• **thread and couch** the leaves and buds

Flowers and stems

1. Follow Fig 2 and first bead the five flowers
marked *, p.82. **Double-stitch** a pearl pink bead
for the centre. **Back-stitch** six or seven cream
pearl beads for the petals (as used here) or try the
quicker method, p.81.

2. Starting at the top, **couch** a single strand of
silver metallic embroidery floss with silver viscose
thread, along the main stem line. **Plunge** the
threads behind the flowers already beaded and
bring them up just in front, see Figs 1, 3 and 4 in
Couching threads.

3. Work the diagonal stems. For the two
horizontal stem lines use *two* adjacent strands.

   It is important to tidy the ends of the metallic
floss on the back of the fabric to avoid a tangle,
see Fig 6 in *Couching threads*.

4. Bead the remaining flowers.

Leaves

5. Leaves are shown on the design by short curved
lines. **Thread and couch** a line of 2 translucent
blue, pink-lined beads.

Buds

6. Buds are shown as pointed ovals. Use the same
method and beads as for leaves, adding a
translucent silver-lined bead at the tip.

Back and lining

The position of these pattern parts should already
have been outlined on the silk.

7. Remove the embroidery from the hoop, but
don't cut out any of the pattern parts yet. For
construction see *Making up*, and for **twisted cord**
see *Edgings*.

Bodkin and needle holder

Worked by the author from a design by
Pam Hancock

*The bellows-shaped bodkin and needle holder
was a popular accessory in Victorian times and
originals can still be found at antiques fairs.
A bodkin would be used for drawing a ribbon
through a hem or eyelets, e.g. in lingerie.*

*Here the front and back flaps are linked by a
hinge and tied at the top. Inside a fine felt leaf
holds a selection of needles. The bodkin is held
in place between the two boards of the back flap.
Recommended for more experienced
embroiderers.*

See Plates 9 and 10 for practice pieces.

You will need

Embroidery hoop 18 cm (7 in), tracing paper and
HB pencil, tissue paper and white dressmaker's
carbon paper. Embroidery needles sizes 8 and 12
and short beading needles size 12.
Fabric. Fine plain mid-red Indian silk, minimum
25 cm (10 in) square. Same amount of fine iron-
on interlining, e.g. vilene softline or pellon.
Threads. Single strand of gold metallic cord, gold
100% viscose thread; blue Nymo* beading thread
gauge D, or polyester thread.
Beads. Seed beads: all size 15°, opaque turquoise,
translucent blue-green, and translucent gold-
lined.

Construction. See *Making
up – bodkin and needle
holders.*

* Nymo beading threads are
sold in the UK without
reference numbers. They must
be conditioned before use by
thorough stretching, to make
them pliable and maintain an
even tension.

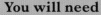

Bodkin and needle holder

Embroidered with seed beads, size 15°, on fine plain mid-red
Indian silk.

Stems are in gold metallic cord couched with gold viscose
thread.

Flower centres are in translucent gold-lined beads; *petals* in
opaque turquoise; *leaves* and *buds* in translucent blue-green
beads, with an opaque turquoise bead at the tip of each bud.

Edging and *ties* are twisted cord in four strands of red
embroidery silk.

The reproduction silver bodkin, 83 mm (3¼ in) long
(see *Suppliers*), is held in place between the two panels
of the back flap. Actual size.

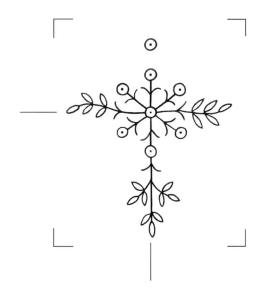

1. Embroidery outline for bodkin holder
Solid lines show stems, circles indicate flowers. The short curved offshoots indicate leaves, and oval shapes the buds.

Carefully trace the outline, locating lines and corner marks, see *Preparing to embroider*. Actual size.

Stitches
Beading 6- to 8-petal flowers, couching metallic thread, threading and couching beads, single-stitching a bead.

All stitches and techniques are shown in the Embroidery notes in **bold italics** and, together with *Starting and fastening off threads* and directions for *Making up* will be found in the Techniques section, or on specified pages and Figures. You may need to refer to them while working the project.

Embroidery notes
Trace the embroidery outline, Fig 1, and transfer it and the pattern parts on to the silk, following the procedure on p.67. This includes mounting the fabric on to the hoop, ready for embroidery.

FRONT
Work in the following stages:
- bead the flowers lying directly across a stem
- **couch** the main stem, then the shorter stems
- work the remaining flowers
- **thread and couch** the leaves and buds

Flowers and stems
1. Follow Fig 2 and Pl 1. Starting at the top, bead the two flowers marked *, see p.82. **Double-stitch** a translucent gold-lined bead in the centre. Then **back-stitch** 6 opaque turquoise beads for the petals (as used here) or try the **quicker method**, p.81.
2. Also from the top, **couch** the metallic cord along the main stem, **plunging** the cord and couching thread behind the flowers already beaded and bringing them up again just in front, see Figs 3 and 4 in *Couching threads*. Work the remaining stems. It is important to tidy the ends of metallic threads on the back of the fabric to avoid a tangle, see Fig 6 in *Couching threads*.
3. Bead the remaining flowers.

Leaves
4. They are shown as short curved lines in Fig 1. **Thread and couch** the lines of translucent blue-green beads for the leaves, and the buds, adding the opaque turquoise bead at the tip.

BACK PANELS AND LININGS
The position of these pattern parts should already have been outlined on the silk.
5. Remove the embroidery from the hoop, but don't cut out any pattern parts yet.
For construction see *Making up*, and for the **twisted cord** see *Edgings*.

2. Guide to beading

Key

Lines – metallic cord
  curved and straight lines – stems: single strand gold metallic
  cord couched with viscose thread.
Circles – seed beads, all size 15°
  heavier circles – centres of flowers: translucent gold-lined.
  solid circles – rings of petals, tips of buds: opaque turquoise.
  fine circles – leaves and buds: translucent blue green.
Starting from the top, embroider the two flowers marked *,
p.82. Now, also from the top, **couch** the main stem, **plunging**
the cord and the couching thread behind the flowers already
worked and bringing them up again in front. Couch the
remaining stems. Bead the remaining flowers. **Thread and
couch** the lines of beads for the leaves, then the buds, adding
the gold bead at the tip.

Pl 1. Enlarged detail of centre

Thimble slipper

Designed and worked by the author

Thimble cases have been produced commercially for several centuries, but cases in the form of a slipper were made by Victorian ladies at home. These would often be attractively embroidered with beads.

Recommended for more experienced embroiderers.

You will need

Embroidery hoop, 18 cm (7 in), tracing paper and HB pencil, tissue paper and white dressmaker's carbon paper. Embroidery needles sizes 8 and 12 and short beading needles size 12.

Fabric. Fine plain Burgundy Indian silk, 25 cm (10 in) square. Same amount of fine iron-on interlining, e.g. vilene softline or pellon.

Threads. Single strand of gold metallic cord, gold 100% viscose thread, grey Nymo* beading thread gauge D, or polyester thread. Charcoal grey embroidery silk for twisted cord.

Beads. Seed beads: size 11°, pearl pink; size 15°, pearl ivory, gun-metal grey and mat gold.

Construction. See *Making up – thimble slippers.*

* Nymo beading threads are sold in the UK without reference numbers. They must be conditioned before use by thorough stretching, to make them pliable and maintain an even tension.

Stitches

Beading 6- to 8-petal flowers, couching metallic thread, threading and couching beads, single-stitching a bead.

All stitches and techniques are shown in the Embroidery notes in **bold italics** and, together with *Starting and fastening off threads* and directions for *Making up* will be found in the Techniques section, or on specified pages and Figures. You may need to refer to them while working the project.

Embroidery notes

Trace the embroidery outline, Fig 1, and transfer it and the pattern parts on to silk, following the

Thimble slipper

Embroidered with seed beads, sizes 15° and 11° on plain fine Burgundy Indian silk.

Stems are in gold metallic cord couched with gold viscose thread.

Flower centres are in pearl pink beads, 11°; *petals* in pearl ivory, 15°.

Leaves and *buds* in gun-metal grey, 15°; *bud tips* in mat gold beads, 15°. The twisted cord is charcoal embroidery silk thread.

Silver gilt thimble by James Swann & Son, Warwick. Actual size.

procedure on p.67. This includes mounting the silk on to the hoop, ready for embroidery.

THE UPPER – top part of slipper
Work in the following stages:
- bead the seven flowers lying directly across a stem
- *couch* the left, then the right hand stem and the shorter ones
- work the remaining flowers,
- *thread and couch* the leaves and buds

Flowers and stems
1. Follow Fig 2 and first bead the seven flowers marked *, p.82. *Double-stitch* a pearl pink bead 11° for the centre. Then *back-stitch* 6 or 7 pearl ivory beads, 15° for the ring of petals (as used here) or try the *quicker method*, p.81.
2. Start couching at the top of the left stem line. *Couch* the gold metallic cord with gold viscose thread, *plunging* the cord and thread behind the flowers already beaded and bringing them up again just in front, see Figs 1, 3 and 4 in *Couching threads*.
3. Work the remaining short stem lines.
It is important to tidy the ends of the metallic cord on the back of the fabric to avoid a tangle, see Fig 6 in *Couching threads*.
4. Bead the remaining flowers.

Leaves
5. Leaves are shown on the embroidery outline by short curved lines. *Thread and couch* a line of 2 or 3 gun-metal grey beads, 15°.

Buds
6. Buds are shown as narrow ovals on the embroidery outline. Use the same method as for leaves, adding a mat gold bead 15° at the tip.

SOLE AND LININGS
The position of these pattern parts should already have been outlined on the silk.
7. Remove the embroidery from the hoop, but don't cut out any pattern parts yet. For construction see *Making up*, and for the *twisted cord* see *Edgings*.

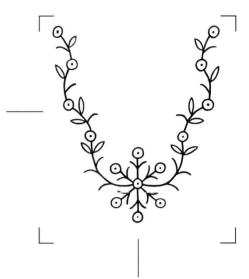

1. Embroidery outline for thimble slipper
Solid lines show stems, circles indicate flowers. The short curved offshoots indicate leaves, and oval shapes the buds.
    Carefully trace the outline, the locating lines and corner marks, see *Preparing to embroider*.
    Actual size.

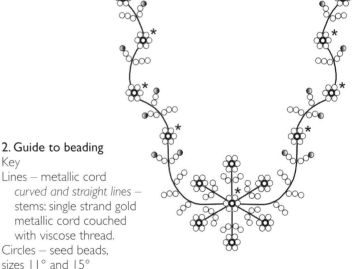

2. Guide to beading
Key
Lines – metallic cord
    curved and straight lines – stems: single strand gold metallic cord couched with viscose thread.
Circles – seed beads, sizes 11° and 15°
    heavier circles – centres of flowers: pearl pink, 11°.
    fine circles – ring of flower petals, leaves and buds: pearl ivory, gun-metal grey, 15°.
    solid circles – tips of buds: mat gold, 15°.
Starting from top left, embroider the seven flowers marked *, p.82. Now, also from top left, *couch* the main stem, *plunging* the cord and the thread behind the flowers already worked and bringing them up again in front. Couch the remaining stems. Bead the remaining flowers. *Thread and couch* the lines of beads for the leaves, then the buds, adding the gold bead at the tip.

2 *From the garden*

Periwinkle
Pincushion with floral border
Pin basket

Periwinkle

Designed and worked by the author

This design with its characteristic triangular petals was inspired by the bead embroidered flowers on a Victorian silk purse.
  The periwinkle is small and quick to work. It can be used for a greetings card, brooch, needle book, or purse. Try experimenting with different backgrounds and sizes of beads, and the practice piece on Plate 9.

Periwinkle

Embroidered with seed beads, sizes 11° and 15°, and silk embroidery floss, on fine plain jade Indian silk.
  The *stalk* is worked in a single strand of green floss.
  The *Flower centre* is a pearl white seed bead, 11°, surrounded by five triangular petals in blue silver-lined beads, 15°. *Leaves* are green silver-lined beads, 15°. Actual size.

You will need

Embroidery hoop, 10 cm (4 in), tracing paper and HB pencil, tissue paper and coloured dressmaker's carbon paper. Embroidery needles size 12, and short beading needles size 12.
Fabric. Fine plain jade Indian silk, 20 cm (8 in) square. Same amount of fine iron-on interlining, e.g. vilene softline or pellon.
Threads. Single strand of green silk embroidery floss; Nymo* beading thread gauge D, or polyester thread.
Beads. Seed beads: size 11°, pearl white; size 15°, blue silver-lined.
Construction. See *Making up – simple mounting*
* Nymo beading threads are sold in the UK without reference numbers. They must be conditioned before use by thorough stretching, to make them pliable and maintain an even tension.

Stitches

Stem stitch; double-stitching a bead, single-stitching beads, threading and couching beads.

All stitches are shown in the Embroidery notes in **bold italics** and, together with *Starting and fastening off threads* and directions for *Making up* will be found in the Techniques section, or on specified pages or Figures. You may need to refer to them while working the project.

Embroidery notes

Preparing to embroider
Trace the embroidery outline, Fig 1, taking care to follow closely the even spacing of the petals round the centre. Transfer the tracing on to the silk, following the procedure on p.67. This includes mounting the silk on to the hoop, ready for embroidery.

FRONT
Work in the following stages:
• ***stem-stitch*** the stalk
• bead the flower
• ***thread and couch*** the leaves

Flower

1. *Stalk*. Starting from the base, ***stem-stitch*** the stalk with the green silk floss, Fig 2.
2. *Centre of flower*. ***Double-stitch*** the single pearl white bead, 11°, in the centre.
3. *The petals*. Use blue silver-lined beads, 15° and follow Figs 2 and 3. Starting from the centre, build up the ring of five petals in three concentric layers. Note the spacing and angles of the beads shown in Fig 3 to create their triangular shape.

Leaves

4. Work the leaves by ***threading and couching*** 2 or 3 green silver-lined beads, 15°, see Fig 2.

5. Remove the embroidery from the hoop, but don't cut it out yet. For construction see *Making up*.

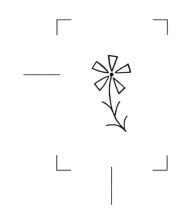

1. Embroidery outline for periwinkle
Lines show the stalk and leaves, the dot is the flower centre and the five triangles are its petals.

Carefully trace the outline, the locating lines and corner marks, see *Preparing to embroider*. Actual size.

2. Guide to beading and embroidery ▶
Key
Line – silk embroidery floss
  curved line – stalk: stem stitch with single strand green silk floss.
Circles – seed beads, sizes 11° and 15°
  heavier circle – flower centre: pearl white seed bead, 11°.
  fine circles – petals in blue silver-lined; leaves in green silver-lined, 15°.
Start by working the stalk in *stem stitch*. Next work the flower, referring to Fig 3: *double-stitch* the centre bead; *single-stitch* 5 single beads round the centre, spacing them evenly, then *straight-stitch* five sets of 2 beads alongside them, carefully maintaining the triangular outline of the petals; finally single stitch five sets of three beads. *Thread and couch* the leaves.

3. Angles of beads on the petals ▶
The bead hole positions show the angles for attaching the beads.

Starting from the centre, build up the ring of five petals in three concentric layers: first *single-stitch* the inner ring of five single beads. Next, *straight-stitch* five sets of two beads; position them carefully to create the beginning of the triangular shape of the petals. Finally straight-stitch the outer ring of five sets of three beads.

If necessary, work *couching stitches* between the beads in the outer sets to keep them in line.

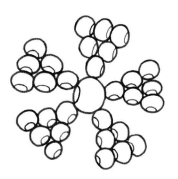

Pin cushion with floral border

Designed and worked by the author

The floral border and special beaded edging which decorate this pin cushion can also be used to great effect on soft furnishings for a doll's house. The pattern can readily be enlarged or reduced and is quite quick to work.

A circular version of the design is also included and could be used as a pin cushion or pin wheel. The embroidery outline for the hat illustrated below is offered for the more adventurous. It too can be worked as a plain round pincushion.

You will need

Embroidery hoop, 15 cm (6 in), tracing paper and HB pencil, tissue paper, white dressmaker's carbon paper. Embroidery needles sizes 8 and 12 and short beading needles size 12.
Fabric. Fine plain deep pink Indian silk, 25 cm (10 in) square. Same amount of iron-on interlining, e.g. vilene softline or pellon.
Threads. Single strand of silver metallic cord, silver 100% viscose thread; grey Nymo* beading thread gauge D, or light grey polyester thread.
Beads. Seed beads: size 11°, frosted pale blue; size 15°, blue-green and translucent silver lined.
Making up. Polyester stuffing, fine sheep's wool or fibrous hamster bedding; sewing thread to match your silk.

* Nymo beading threads are sold in the UK without reference numbers. They must be conditioned before use by thorough stretching, to make them pliable and maintain an even tension.

Stitches

Beading 4-petal flowers, straight-stitching beads, couching metallic thread, flat beaded edging.

All stitches and techniques are shown in the Embroidery notes in **bold italics** and, together with *Starting and fastening off threads* and directions for *Making up* will be found under Techniques, or on specified pages or Figures. You may need to refer to them while working the project.

Embroidery notes

Trace the embroidery outline, Fig 1, and transfer it and the pattern parts on to the silk, following the procedure on p.67. This includes mounting the silk on to the hoop, ready for embroidery.

FRONT
Work in the following stages:
• bead the four-petal flowers, then the leaves
• *couch* the border stem

The border
1. Follow Fig 2 and bead the four-petal flowers, p.80. **Double-stitch** a frosted blue bead 11° for the centre, and **single-stitch** four translucent silver lined beads, 15° for the petals.
2. Embroider the leaves by **straight-stitching** pairs of blue-green beads, 15°. Make the straight stitch long enough so that the beads can lie snugly together. Leave a tiny gap between the bases of the two leaves, just enough to allow the metallic cord to be couched between them without distorting the beads, see Fig 2 in **4-petal flowers**.
3. **Couch** the silver metallic cord with silver viscose thread along the border outline line, between the pairs of leaves, **plunging** the cord and thread behind the already beaded flowers and bringing them up just in front. See Figs 3 and 4 in *Couching threads*, and practice piece Pl 10.

It is important to tidy the ends of the metallic cord on the back of the fabric to avoid a tangle, see Fig 6 in *Couching threads*.

Making up
This project is made up like a miniature cushion. The Back outline is already tacked on the silk.
4. Remove the embroidery from the hoop. Cut out the Front carefully, then the Back.
5. Turn the seam allowances under each edge for Front and Back. Make sure the two match in size, and tack the folded seam allowances on each piece. **Oversew** three edges, insert the stuffing and oversew the fourth edge. Now work the **flat beaded edging** all the way round *on top* of the oversewing.

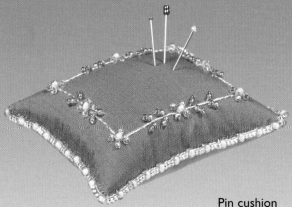

Pin cushion

Embroidered with seed beads, sizes 11° and 15°, on fine plain deep pink Indian silk.

Flower centres are frosted pale blue beads 11°; *petals* are translucent silver-lined beads 15°; *leaves* are blue-green 15°.

The *stem line* is in silver metallic cord couched with silver viscose thread. The *flat beaded edging* is translucent silver-lined and blue-green beads 15°. Actual size.

2. Guide to beading

Key

Lines – silver metallic cord couched with viscose thread
Circles – seed beads: sizes 11° and 15°
   heavier circles – flower centres: frosted pale blue, 11°
   lighter circles – petals, leaves, flat beaded edging: translucent silver-lined, and blue-green, 15°.
Starting from top left embroider the four-petal flowers, p.80. Next **single-stitch** the pairs of beads for the leaves,

leaving a tiny gap, Fig 2 p.80, between their bases for **couching** the metallic cord.

   Beginning at a corner, couch the silver metallic cord with silver viscose thread; **plunge** the cord and thread to the back of the fabric just before a flower already worked and bring it up just beyond it, p.86.

1. Embroidery outline for pin cushion

Lines show border stem line; short lines are leaves; dots indicate flower centres and petals.

   Carefully trace the outline, the locating lines and corner marks, see *Preparing to embroider*. Actual size.

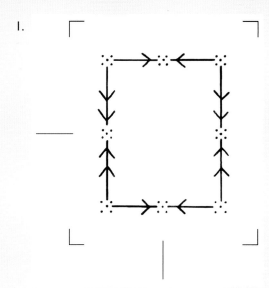

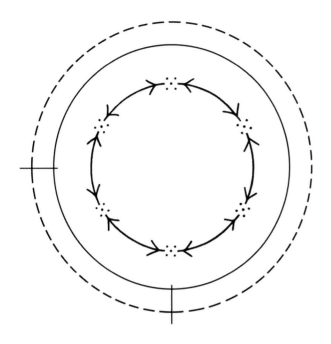

◄ **3. Embroidery and pattern outline for round floral border**
To make a round pin cushion, use this outline but follow the instructions above for the rectangular version. The solid circle shows the edge of the pin cushion and the outer broken circle is the pattern outline.

4. Embroidery outline – Summer hat pin cushion
The circles with dots are flowers, the short lines are flower stalks and leaves, and the wavy continuous line is the stem. The solid circle shows the edge of the hat and the outer broken circle is the pattern outline.

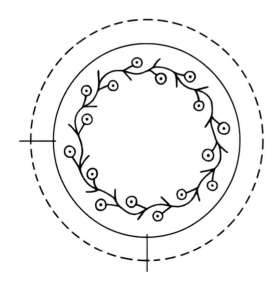

Pl 2. Summer hat pin cushion
Designed and worked by the author.

Based on a Victorian example and worked with seed beads sizes 11° and 15° on fine plain butter-yellow Indian silk. White seed beads 11° form the *flower centres*, with blue silver-lined 15° for the *petals*, worked in the *Standard method for flowers*. Pairs of *straight-stitched* 15° clear silver-lined beads form the *leaves*. The *stem* is two strands of metallic copper floss *couched* with viscose, with metallic copper purl (gimp or bullion) for the *stalks*. The crown and brim are edged with a royal blue silk *twisted cord* matching the silk ribbon. Actual size.

Pin basket

Adapted and worked by the author

This accessory is a close copy of an exquisite antique pin basket seen at a fair.

The project will appeal to more experienced embroiderers who enjoy working in coloured threads as well as beads. You may wish to try different colour combinations of silk and flowers.

You will need

Embroidery hoop 15 cm (6 in), tracing paper and HB pencil, tissue paper and white dressmaker's carbon paper, coloured dressmaker's carbon paper. Embroidery needles size 12 and short beading needles size 12.

Fabric. Fine plain cream Indian silk, 25 cm (10 in) square. Same amount of iron-on fine interlining, e.g. vilene softline or pellon.

Threads. Single strand of pastel green and pea green silk embroidery floss, or stranded embroidery cotton; Nymo* beading thread gauge D, or polyester thread.

Beads. Seed beads: size 11°, yellow; size 15°, turquoise.

Construction. See *Making up – pin basket.*

* Nymo beading threads are sold in the UK without reference numbers. They must be conditioned before use by thorough stretching, to make them pliable and maintain an even tension.

Pin basket

Embroidered with silk floss and seed beads, size 11° and 15°, on plain cream Indian silk.

Leaves and *stems* are pea green and pastel green silk floss, worked in stem and satin stitches.

Flower centres are yellow beads, 11°, *petals* and *buds* in turquoise beads, 15°. The triple bead edging is in opaque white 15°. Actual size.

Stitches

Stem stitch, satin stitch, beading 6- to 8-petal flowers, sewing a bead singly, triple bead edging.

Stitches used only in this design are explained in the Embroidery notes and diagrams and shown in **bold** type.

Stitches used in other projects as well are shown in ***bold italics*** and, together with instructions for *Preparing to embroider*, and for *Making up*, will be found under Techniques or on specified pages or Figures. You may need to refer to them while working the project.

Embroidery notes

Trace the embroidery outline, Fig 1, and transfer it and the pattern parts on to the silk, following the procedure on p.67. This includes mounting the silk on to the hoop, ready for embroidery.

FRONT – *forget-me-nots*

Work from left to right in the following stages:

- start each leaf by **stem-stitching** the central vein
- **satin-stitch** the left half in the same shade as the vein
- satin-stitch the right half in the other shade of green
- work the stems
- bead the flowers and buds

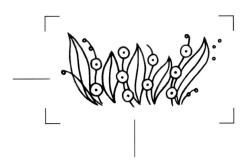

1. Embroidery outline for pin basket

Lines indicate stems, outlines of leaves and centre veins; larger circles indicate flowers, and small circles buds.

Carefully trace the outline, the locating lines and corner marks, see *Starting to embroider*. Actual size.

Leaves

1. Follow Figs 2 to 4 and work each leaf in the above stages.

Note on colour. Work the two halves of all leaves in the contrasting shades of green (here pea green and pastel green), but vary the halves for the light and dark threads. Always use the *same* shade of green for the *central vein* and for the *left half* of the leaf.

2. Starting from the bottom work the centre vein in **stem stitch**, Fig 2.

3. Follow Fig 3 to work the **satin stitches**. Use the diagonal lines as a guide to angle the stitches.

4. Start half-way up the left half, with first stitch *A-B* and work *over* the centre vein down to the base of the leaf. Return just above *A* and complete the left half with satin stitches up to the tip.

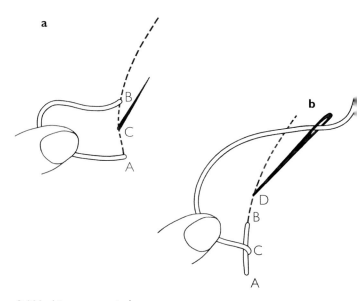

2. Working stem stitch

This will be used for the centre vein in the leaves.

a. The broken line represents the curving stem. Bring up the needle at *A* and take it down at *B* while holding the loop of thread to one side with the left thumb. Now bring the needle up at *C*, release the loop and pull the stitch taut to follow the marked stem line.

b. Insert the needle at *D* and hold the loop once again with your left thumb. Make sure the distance from *B* to *C* is the same as from *B* to *D*. Bring the needle up at *B*, and as the needle emerges pull the loop taut. Continue in this way along the stem line.

5. Repeat for the right half using the contrasting pea green.
Note. When working the right half, take the satin stitches up to the edge of the left half, already covered by satin stitches, but *not over it*.

Stems
6. Embroider the stems in **stem stitch** in pastel green and, where necessary, work over the leaf already completed.

Flowers and buds
7. Work the flowers as directed on p.81, using either the **standard** or the **quicker method**. Some petals will be stitched over leaves already worked. **Single-stitch** individual beads to form buds.

Back
The position of the Back should already have been outlined on the silk. If you plan to work the Back, continue to *8*. Otherwise go to *10*, but don't cut out either pattern part yet.

8. To embroider the Back, remove the silk from the hoop. Transfer the embroidery outline, Fig 1, on to the silk as before, then remount the silk on to the hoop.

9. Work the Back using the same techniques as for the Front, and bead in contrasting colours if you wish.

3. Working satin stitch
The centre vein is shown worked in *stem stitch*.
Bring up the needle about half way up the left edge, at *A*, and insert it over the stem-stitched centre vein, at *B*. Pull the thread taut to make stitch A-B. Bring up the needle at *C*, beside *A*, and take it down at *D*, beside *B*, to make an adjacent *satin stitch*.

Continue working in satin stitch down to the base of the leaf, using the diagonal lines as a guide to angle the stitches and inserting the needle over the worked central vein. Take the thread to the back of the fabric and through the stitches and bring up the needle just above *A*. Now work satin stitches up to the tip of the leaf. Tidy the thread ends at the back of the fabric by securing the working thread through the satin stitches, and trim.
Note. For best results always insert the needle vertically through the fabric.

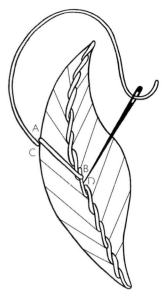

10. Remove the embroidery from the hoop. For construction see *Making up*, and for **triple bead edging** see *Edgings*.

4. Guide to embroidery and beading
Key
Lines – silk embroidery floss
   centre lines of leaves – centre vein: stem stitch in same shade as left half of leaf.
   finer diagonal lines – direction of satin stitches: pastel green or pea green.
   single heavier lines – flower stems, stem stitch: pea green.
Circles – seed beads, sizes 11° and 15°
   heavier circles – flower centres: yellow seed beads, 11°.
   finer circles – petals and buds: turquoise seed beads, 15°.
Work the central vein of leaves in *stem stitch* and their surface in *satin stitch*; then work the stems in stem stitch. Bead embroider the flowers, p.81. *Single-stitch* the beads for the buds.

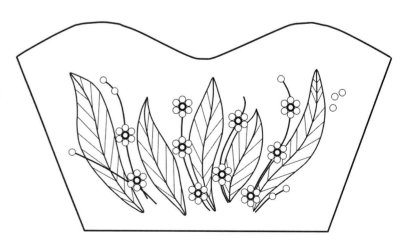

3 *Beaded lotus*

Needle book
Bodkin and needle holder
Pin wheel
Thimble slipper

Needle book

Designed and worked by the author

The pattern was inspired by motifs from hand-embroidered dresses from the Indian sub continent. The design is symmetrical and its focal point is a stylised eight-petal lotus blossom, which features in much Eastern decorative art.

The project is recommended for more experienced embroiderers.

You will need

Embroidery hoop 18 cm (7 in), tracing paper and HB pencil, tissue paper and white dressmaker's carbon paper. Short beading needles size 12, embroidery needles sizes 8 and 12.
Fabric. Plain fine mauve Indian silk, minimum 25 cm (10 in) square. Same amount of fine iron-on interlining, e.g. vilene softline or pellon.
Threads. Nymo* mauve beading thread gauge D; gold metallic** cord, gold 100% viscose thread; smooth metallic purl (gimp or bullion), size 9.
Beads. Seed beads: size 11°, opaque gold and frosted green; size 15°, translucent purple foil-lined, and opaque gold.
Bugle beads: size 3 mm (⅛ in), bronzed metallic-purple, and mat teal green.
Construction. See *Making up – needle books.*

* Nymo beading threads are sold in the UK without reference numbers. They must be conditioned before use by thorough stretching, to make them pliable and maintain an even tension.
** Metallic thread, especially purl, will blunt sharp scissors. Try using a craft knife on felt covered board.

Stitches

Stitches unique to the Lotus designs are shown in the Embroidery notes in **bold type** and explained in *Stitches used,* p.47.

Stitches used for other designs as well are shown in ***bold italics,*** and together with guidance on *Starting and fastening off threads* and instructions for *Making up,* will be found under Techniques, or on specified pages or Figures. You may need to refer to them while working the project.

2. Guide to beading

Key

Circles – seed beads, sizes 11° and 15°
  heavier circles – centre of lotus flower and its stamens; centre and base of the buds; centres of corner flowers: opaque gold, frosted green, 11°.
  fine circles – ring of beads in centre of lotus flower; tips of leaves and stamen tips of corner flowers, petals of buds, picot edging: translucent purple, opaque gold, 15°.
Rectangles within ovals – bugle beads
  rectangles – surface of petals and leaves: bronzed metallic purple, mat teal green, size 3 mm (⅛ in).
Lines – couched metallic cord, stitched metallic purl
  fine lines, curved with scroll or straight – stems and tendrils: couched gold cord.
  oval pointed outlines – petal and leaf edging: two lengths of purl, Figs 2 and 3, p.47.
  heavier curved, or tiny straight lines – base and tip of bud (calyx): purl, Fig 4, p.49.
Start with the lotus flower, then ***couch*** the stems and embroider the leaves; work the corner flowers, and finally the two buds flanking the lotus. See *Stitches used,* p.47.

Embroidery notes

Trace the embroidery outline, Fig 1 (*see next page*), and transfer it and the pattern parts on to the silk, following the procedure on p.67. This includes mounting the silk on to the hoop, ready for embroidery.

Tracing and transferring the embroidery outline needs to be done carefully, especially the curved lines, to maintain the symmetry of the design.

FRONT
Work in the following stages:

- embroider the lotus flower
- *couch* the stems, and embroider the leaves
- work the corner flowers
- work the two buds flanking the lotus flower

Lotus flower

1. This is the focal point of the design. Follow Fig 2 opposite, and Figs 1-3 on p.82. Start in the middle and *double-stitch* the single opaque gold seed bead, 11°. Then *back-stitch* eight 15° translucent purple beads around it.

Lotus needle book

Embroidered with seed beads, sizes 11° and 15°, 3 mm (⅛ in) bugle beads, metallic cord and smooth metallic purl size 9, on fine plain mauve Indian silk.

Stems and tendrils are in gold metallic cord couched with viscose thread.

The *flower* has at its centre an opaque gold bead, 11°, and eight translucent purple beads, 15°. *Petals* are 3 mm (⅛ in) bronzed metallic-purple bugle beads, edged with purl. *Stamens* are opaque gold beads, 11°.

Corner flowers and *leaves* are bronzed metallic-purple and mat teal green bugle beads. *Stamens* are translucent purple beads, *tips of leaves* are opaque gold beads, 15°.

The *bud sprigs* consist of gold metallic cord, 11° opaque gold and two translucent purple beads, 15°. The *bud* itself comprises a frosted green bead, 11°, enclosed by metallic purl and four translucent purple beads, 15°, with a tiny purl tip.

The *picot edging* is in mat gold and translucent purple beads, 15°.

The interior is lined with mauve silk paper, and a folded piece of fine cream wool provides the needle pages, see Pl 12. Actual size.

Work the petals with 3 mm (⅛ in) bronzed metallic-purple bugle beads, and **edge** them with purl. Finally *double-stitch* eight opaque gold seed beads, 11°, on a circle defined by the tips of the petals.

Stems

2. **Couch** the gold metallic cord along the stem lines with gold viscose. The tight curves at the tips of stems need special attention. To create them accurately use the closer couching stitches described in **couching a tight scroll**. Also, it is important to tidy the ends of metallic cord on the back of the fabric to avoid a tangle, see Fig 6, p.88.

continued overleaf

1. Embroidery outline for Lotus needle book
Straight and curved lines indicate stems. Tightly curved lines on the flower buds, with a dot, show tendrils. Other dots indicate smaller stamens, and leaf tips.

Circles show flower and bud centres, and larger stamens. The larger circle in the middle of the lotus flower is the ring of small petals round the centre. Pointed ovals indicate petals and leaves.

The outer halves of the broken circles on the bud motif indicate the closed petals, the inner shows the base of the bud.

Tracing and transferring the outline needs to be done carefully, especially the curved lines, to maintain the symmetry of the design. Trace the outline, together with the locating lines and corner marks, see *Preparing to embroider*. Actual size.

Leaves

3. Embroider the leaves as you did the petals of the lotus flower, but use mat teal green bugle beads, Figs 2 and 3, p.47.

The dot on the tips of some leaves is an opaque gold seed bead. Thread on the bead *before* completing the couching of the purl edging, see Fig 4, p.48.

Corner flowers

4. Use the same techniques for the petals as for the central lotus flower, p.47. **Double-stitch** an 11° opaque gold seed bead at the centre of each corner flower, and **single-stitch** a 15° translucent purple bead for each stamen tip.

Bud sprigs

Work the sprigs on either side of the lotus flower in the following order:
• couch the tendrils and the straight stem
• work the bud centre and its base (calyx)
• bead the petals and tips, the base of the stem, and each tendril coil.

5. *Tendrils and stem.* Follow Fig 2, p.36, and Fig 1, p.49. **Couch** the gold metallic cord with gold viscose along the tendrils and stem lines.

Start at *A* and follow the order of lettering to *F*. The larger steps, from *B* to *C* and *D* to *E*, are to avoid too close stitching which can damage the silk. To create the **tight curves** of the coiled tips work the couching stitches closer together. Tension them well by using **knotting stitches** on the back of the fabric, placing them so they don't distort the smooth surface.

6. *The bud.* Work the bud itself in four stages, Figs 2 to 4, p.49. First **double-stitch** the 11° frosted green bead in the middle. Secure the purl round the base of the bud (calyx). **Thread and couch** a line of four 15° translucent purple beads for the petals, and complete the bud with a **purl stitch** at the tip, securing it between the two middle beads.

7. *Beading the base of the stem and tendril coils.* **Double-stitch** an 11° opaque gold bead at the base of the stem and **single-stitch** a 15° translucent purple seed bead in the coiled tips of the leaves.

Back and spine

The position of these pattern parts should already have been outlined on the silk.

8. Remove the embroidery from the hoop, but don't cut out any pattern parts yet.

For construction see *Making up*, and for **picot edging** see *Edgings*.

Bodkin & needle holder

Adapted and worked by Pam Hancock

This bellows-shaped 19th century accessory can sometimes be found at antiques fairs. Bodkins were used for threading ribbons, in lingerie for example, and were a common item in ladies' sewing boxes.

The design, with its eight-petal lotus flower, was inspired by motifs on hand-embroidered dresses from the Indian sub continent.

Recommended for more experienced embroiderers, but a simpler embroidery on the same popular bellows shape can be found among the Victorian style projects.

Lotus bodkin holder

Embroidered with seed beads, sizes 11° and 15°, 3 mm (⅛ in) bugle beads and smooth metallic purl on fine plain apple-green Indian silk.

The *flower centre* is a mat gold bead, 11°, with eight translucent blue pink-lined seed beads, 15°. *Petals* are 3 mm (⅛ in) metallic and mat purple bugle beads, edged with purl. *Stamens* are mat gold seed beads, 15°.

The *bud sprigs* consist of a stem and tendrils, made of metallic floss with an 11° and two 15° mat gold beads, and the *bud* itself. The bud comprises a frosted green bead 11°, enclosed by purl and translucent blue pink-lined beads 15°, with a tiny purl tip.

The *picot edging* is in mat gold and translucent blue pink-lined beads, 15°.

The *flower* on the silk tie is a frosted green bead 11°, with eight translucent blue pink-lined beads 15°. The bodkin is held in place between the two components of the back flap. Actual size.

You will need

Embroidery hoop 18 cm (7 in), tracing paper and HB pencil, tissue paper and white dressmaker's carbon paper. Short beading needles, size 12, embroidery needles sizes 8 and 12.

Fabric. Fine plain apple-green Indian silk, minimum 25 cm (10 in) square. Same amount of fine iron-on interlining, e.g. vilene softline or pellon.

Threads. Nymo* mauve beading thread gauge D, or polyester thread; two adjacent strands of gold stranded metallic** floss, gold 100% viscose thread; smooth metallic purl (gimp or bullion), size 9.

Beads. Seed beads: size 11°, mat gold, frosted green; size 15°, translucent blue pink-lined and mat gold. Bugle beads: size 3 mm (⅛ in), metallic purple.

Construction. See *Making up – bodkin & needle holders.*

* Nymo beading threads are sold in the UK without reference numbers. They must be conditioned before use by thorough stretching, to make them pliable and maintain an even tension.

** Metallic thread, especially purl, will blunt sharp scissors. Try using a craft knife on felt covered board.

Stitches

Beading the lotus flower, making a tiny stitch with purl, couching metallic thread including tight scrolls, knotting stitches, picot edging.

Stitches unique to the Lotus designs are shown in the Embroidery notes in **bold** type and explained in *Stitches used*, p.47.

Stitches and techniques used for other designs as well are shown in ***bold italics*** and, together with guidance on *Starting and fastening off threads* and instructions for *Making up*, will be found under Techniques, or on specified pages or Figures. You may need to refer to them while working the project.

1. Embroidery outline for Lotus bodkin holder

Straight lines indicate stems; the two tightly curved lines on each bud are tendrils. Dots round the central flower are stamens.

Circles show flower and bud centres. The larger circle in the middle of the lotus flower is the ring of small petals round the centre. Pointed ovals are the lotus petals.

The outer halves of the broken circles on the bud motif indicate the closed petals, the inner show the base of the bud (calyx).

Tracing and transferring the outline needs to be done carefully, especially the curved lines, to maintain the symmetry of the design. Trace the outline, the locating lines and corner marks, see *Preparing to embroider*. Actual size.

Embroidery notes

Trace the embroidery outline, Fig 1, and transfer it and the pattern parts on to the silk, following the procedure on p.67. This includes mounting the silk on to the hoop, ready for embroidery.

Tracing and transferring the embroidery outline needs to be done carefully, especially of the curved lines, to maintain the symmetry of the design.

FRONT

Work in the following stages:
* embroider the lotus flower
* work the three buds
* on completion secure the ties with an embroidered flower

Lotus flower

1. Start with the lotus flower. Follow Fig 2 and Pl 3, and Figs 1 to 3 on p.47. Begin in the middle and ***double-stitch*** the single mat gold seed bead, 11°. Then ***back-stitch*** eight 15° translucent blue pink-lined beads around it.

Embroider the petals with 3 mm (⅛ in) purple bugle beads, and **edge** them with purl. Finally ***double-stitch*** the eight mat gold seed beads, 11°, on a circle defined by the tips of the petals.

Bud sprigs

Work the sprigs in the following order:
* couch the tendrils and the stem
* work the bud centre and its base (calyx)
* bead the petals and tips, the base of the stem and each tendril coil.

2. *Tendrils and stem*. Follow Fig 2 and Pl 3, and Fig 1, p.48. ***Couch*** the metallic floss with gold viscose along the tendrils and stem outlines.

It is important to tidy the ends of metallic floss on the back of the fabric to avoid a tangle, see Fig 6 in *Couching threads*.

To create the **tight curves** of the coiled tips work the couching stitches closer together. Tension them well by using ***knotting stitches*** on the back of the fabric, placing them so they don't distort the smooth surface.

3. *The bud.* Work the bud itself in four stages, Figs 2 to 4, p.49.
- **Double-stitch** the 11° frosted green bead in the middle
- **Edge** it with purl to form the base of the bud (calyx)
- **Thread and couch** a line of four 15° translucent blue pink-lined beads
- Complete the bud with a **tiny stitch** of purl at the top, securing it between the two middle beads.

4. *Base of the stem and tendril coils.* **Double-stitch** an 11° mat gold bead at the base of the stem and **single-stitch** a 15° mat gold bead in the coiled tips of the tendrils.

BACK, HINGE AND LINING
The position of these pattern parts should already have been outlined on the silk.
5. Remove the embroidery from the hoop, but don't cut out any pattern parts yet. For construction see *Making up*, and for **picot edging** see *Edgings*.

Pl 3. Detail of centre and bud sprigs. Enlarged.

2. Guide to beading
Key
Circles – seed beads, sizes 11° and 15°
  heavier circles – centre of lotus flower, base and centre of buds: mat gold, frosted green 11°.
  fine circles – ring of petals round centre of lotus flower and its stamen; tips of tendrils and bud petals; picot edging: translucent blue pink-lined, mat gold 15°.
Rectangles within ovals – bugle beads
  rectangles – surface of petals: metallic and mat purple-green bugle beads, 3 mm (⅛ in).
Lines – couched in two strands of metallic floss; smooth purl, size 9.
  fine lines, curved or straight – stems and tendrils: two strands of couched metallic floss.
  oval pointed outlines – edging of petals: two pieces of smooth purl, Figs 2 to 3, p.47.
  heavier curved, or very short straight lines – base of bud (calyx) and tip: smooth purl, Fig 4, p.49.
Start with the lotus flower then embroider the bud sprigs, starting on the left. Follow *Stitches used* Figs 1 to 4, p.49. See also *Couching metallic threads*.

Pin wheel

Designed and worked by the author

A pin wheel was one of the needlework accessories often found in traditional sewing boxes. This pattern was inspired by the stylised lotus flower carved on a 19th century ivory pin wheel, shown below.

The project is recommended for those already familiar with bead embroidery.

You will need

Embroidery hoop 15 cm (6 in), tracing paper and HB pencil, tissue paper and blue dressmaker's carbon paper. Short beading needles size 12, embroidery needles sizes 8 and 12.

Fabric. Plain fine saffron gold Indian silk, 25 cm (10 in) square. Same amount of fine iron-on interlining, e.g. vilene softline or pellon.

Threads. Nymo* gold beading thread gauge D; gold smooth metallic** purl (gimp or bullion), size 9; gold 100% viscose.

Beads. Seed beads: size 11°, mat gold, translucent blue foil-lined; size 15°, mat gold and translucent blue foil-lined. Bugle beads: size 3 mm (⅛ in), iridescent blue.

Construction. See *Making up – pin wheels.*

* Nymo beading threads are sold in the UK without reference numbers. They must be conditioned before use by thorough stretching.

** Metallic thread, especially purl, will blunt sharp scissors. Try using a craft knife on felt covered board.

Antique ivory pin wheel with bead embroidered version
The stylised 8-petal lotus flower and stamens, and the beaded edging, are reproduced in silk and beads for this project.

Embroidered on fine plain gold Indian silk with seed beads sizes 11° and 15°, bugle beads, and smooth metallic purl.

The *centre of the lotus* is an 11° mat gold bead with a ring of eight translucent blue foil-lined beads, 15°. *Petals* are 3 mm (⅛ in) iridescent blue bugle beads, edged with metallic purl. *Stamen tips* are mat gold beads, 15°. The edging is sixteen translucent blue foil-lined beads, 11°. The middle is felt padded to hold the pins and edged with a ribbon. A gold twisted cord is stitched round both edges.

The design is repeated on the Back with translucent green foil-lined and mat gold seed beads, and iridescent green bugle beads. Actual size.

Stitches

Beading the lotus flower, single-stitching a bead, twisted cord.

Stitches unique to the Lotus designs are shown in the Embroidery notes in **bold type** and explained in detail in *Stitches used*, p.47.

Stitches used for other designs as well, are shown in ***bold italics*** and, together with guidance on *Starting and fastening off threads* and instructions for *Making up,* will be found under Techniques, or on specified pages or Figures. You may have to refer to them while working the project.

Embroidery notes

Trace the embroidery outline, Fig 1, and transfer it and the pattern parts on to the silk, following the procedure on p.67. This includes mounting the silk on to the hoop, ready for embroidery.

Tracing and transferring the embroidery outline needs to be done carefully, especially the curved outlines and the spacing between the single beads, to maintain the symmetry of the design.

FRONT
Work in the following stages:
- embroider the lotus flower
- *double-stitch* the beads round the edge

Lotus flower
1. Follow Fig 2 below, and Figs 1 to 3 on p.47. Start in the middle and *double-stitch* the single mat gold seed bead, 11°. Then *back-stitch* eight 15° translucent blue foil-lined beads around it.

Work the **lotus** petals with 3 mm (⅛ in) iridescent blue bugle beads; **edge** them with purl. Double-stitch eight mat gold seed beads, 15°, on the outer circle defined by the tips of the petals.

Outer ring of 16 beads
2. Ensure the silk is held taut in the hoop. Sew the 16 translucent blue foil-lined beads, 11°, securing each with a well tensioned double-stitch. Work a *knotting stitch* over the threads of each double-stitch and continue to the next bead without cutting off the thread.

BACK
The position of the Back should already have been outlined on the silk. If you plan to embroider the Back, proceed to *3*. Otherwise go to *5*, but don't cut out either pattern part yet.
3. To embroider the Back, remove the silk from the hoop. Transfer the embroidery outline, Fig 1, on to the silk as before, then mount the silk back on to the hoop.
4. Work the Back with the same techniques as the Front, and bead in contrasting colours if you wish.
5. Remove the embroidery from the hoop. For construction see *Making up*, and for *twisted cord* see *Edgings*.

1. Embroidery outline for Lotus pin wheel

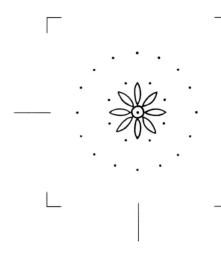

The central dot shows the centre of the lotus flower. The circle round it represents the inner ring of petals. The pointed ovals are the outer petals, edged with smooth metallic purl. Dots between petals are stamen tips. The 16 dots round the edge reproduce the beading round the ivory original.

Tracing and transferring the outline needs to be done carefully, especially the curved lines, to maintain the symmetry of the design. Trace the outline and the locating lines, see *Preparing to embroider*. Actual size.

2. Guide to beading
Key
Circles — seed beads, sizes 11° and 15°
  heavier circles — centre of lotus flower and ring of beads round the edge: mat gold, translucent blue foil-lined, 11°.
  fine circles — ring of beads in centre and stamen tips: translucent blue foil-lined, mat gold, 15°.
Rectangles within ovals — bugle beads
  rectangles — surface of petals: iridescent blue, 3 mm (⅛ in).
  oval outlines — petal edging: two lengths of smooth metallic purl, size 9. Figs 2 to 3, p.47.
Embroider the lotus flower: *double-stitch* the centre bead, then *back-stitch* eight beads round it, between adjacent petals, as shown. Bead and edge the petals, then the stamen tips. Double-stitch 16 beads evenly round the outer edge.

Thimble slipper

Designed and worked by the author

Among the thimble cases traditionally found in Ladies' sewing boxes were some shaped as miniature footwear. These would often be made at home, demonstrating the needlewoman's skill.

Here the beaded lotus motif has been adapted to create a sparkling slipper. The project is recommended for more experienced embroiderers.

You will need

Embroidery hoop 18 cm (7 in), tracing paper and HB pencil, tissue paper and white dressmaker's carbon paper. Short beading needles size 12, embroidery needles, sizes 8 and 12.
Fabric. Fine plain mauve Indian silk, minimum 25 cm (10 in) square. Same amount of fine iron-on interlining, e.g. vilene softline or pellon.
Threads. Nymo* mauve beading thread gauge D, or polyester thread; single strand of gold metallic** cord, gold 100% viscose; smooth metallic purl (gimp or bullion), size 9.
Beads. Seed beads: size 11°, opaque gold and frosted green; size 15°, translucent purple foil-lined and opaque gold. Bugle beads: size 3 mm (⅛ in), bronzed metallic-purple, and mat teal green.
Construction. See *Making up – thimble slippers.*

* Nymo beading threads are sold in the UK without reference numbers. They must be conditioned before use by thorough stretching.
** Metallic thread, especially purl, will blunt sharp scissors. Try using a craft knife on felt covered board.

Stitches

Beading the lotus flower, couching metallic thread including tight scrolls, knotting stitches, single-stitching a bead, twisted cord.

Stitches unique to the Lotus designs are shown in the Embroidery notes in **bold type** and explained in *Stitches used*, p.47.

Stitches used for other designs as well are shown in ***bold italics*** and, together with guidance on *Starting and fastening off stitches* and directions for *Making up*, will be found under Techniques, or on specified pages or Figures. You may need to refer to them while working the project.

Lotus thimble slipper
The project makes a companion piece to the *Lotus needle book*, p.36. It uses the same materials, but the frosted green beads of the bud centres on the needle book are used here both for the diamond frame surrounding the lotus, and for the three embellishments on each side of the slipper.

Silver gilt thimble, set with amethysts, by James Swann & Son, Warwick. Actual size.

Embroidery notes

Trace the embroidery outline, Fig 1 (*on p.46*), and transfer it and the pattern parts on to the silk, following the procedure on p.67. This includes mounting the silk on to the hoop, ready for embroidery.

Tracing and transferring the embroidery outline needs to be done carefully, especially the curved lines, to maintain the symmetry of the design.

THE UPPER – top part of slipper
Work in the following stages:
- embroider the lotus flower
- **couch** the stems and tight curves
- embroider the leaves
- **double-stitch** the single beads at the front and sides

Lotus flower
This is the focal point of the design. Follow Fig 2, and Figs 1 to 3 on p.47.
1. Start in the middle and **double-stitch** the single opaque gold seed bead, 11°. Then **back-stitch** eight 15° translucent purple beads around it.

Work the petals with 3 mm (⅛ in) bronzed metallic-purple bugle beads; **edge** them with metallic purl. Double-stitch the eight opaque gold seed beads, 15°, on the outer circle defined by the tips of the petals.

Stems and leaves
2. *Stems.* Starting from the top left sprig, work towards you.

Couch the gold metallic cord along the stem lines with gold viscose. It is important to tidy the ends of metallic cord on the back of the fabric to avoid a tangle, see Fig 6, p.88.

The tight scrolls at the tips of stems need special attention. To create them accurately use the closer couching stitches described in working **tight scrolls**, Fig 1, p.48, together with **knotting stitches**. Repeat for the right-hand side.
3. *Leaves.* Follow Figs 2 to 4, pp.47-48. Bead the leaves in the same way as the petals of the lotus flower, but use mat teal green bugle beads.

2. Guide to beading

Key
Circles – seed beads, sizes 11° and 15°
heavier circles – centre and corners of lotus flower, and single bead embellishments on the sides: opaque gold, green frosted, 11°.
fine circles – ring of beads in centre of lotus flower, its stamens, and the tips of leaves: translucent purple, opaque gold, 15°.
Rectangles within ovals – bugle beads
rectangles – surface of petals and leaves: bronzed metallic purple, mat teal green, 3 mm (⅛ in).
Lines – couched metallic cord, smooth purl
fine lines with a scroll – stems: gold metallic cord couched with viscose thread.
oval pointed outlines – petal and leaf edging: two lengths of smooth gold purl, size 9.
Follow Figs 2 to 4, pp.47-48, and start with the lotus flower. Work the centre, then a petal and a stamen, and work in this order round the flower. No need to cut off between stages. **Couch** the stems and embroider the leaves. **Double-stitch** the flower corner beads and single bead embellishments on the sides.

continued overleaf

Use opaque gold seed beads 15° for the tips of leaves. Secure each with a ***single stitch***. Thread the bead *before* completing the couching of the purl edging.

Embellishments
4. Double-stitch a frosted green seed bead, 11°, at each corner of the diamond shape framing the lotus flower, and 3 on either side of the Upper.

SOLE AND LININGS
The position of the remaining pattern parts: the lining of the Upper, the Sole and its lining, should already have been outlined on the silk, Pl 7.

5. Remove the embroidery from the hoop, but don't cut out any pattern parts yet.
For construction see *Making up,* and for ***twisted cord*** see *Edgings.*

1. Embroidery outline for Lotus thimble slipper
Curved/scrolled lines indicate stems. The small circles indicate the flower centre and corners, and side embellishments. The larger circle in the middle of the lotus flower represents a ring of small petals. Dots indicate the flower stamens and leaf tips. Pointed ovals indicate petals and leaves.

Tracing and transferring the outline needs to be done carefully, especially the curved lines, to maintain the symmetry of the design. Trace the outline, the locating lines and corner marks, see *Preparing to embroider.* Actual size.

Stitches in lotus projects

The Beaded lotus projects have their own special stitches: stitching bugle beads, edging petals and leaves with purl (gimp or bullion), adding a single bead to a leaf tip, couching metallic thread round tight scrolls, and making a small stitch with purl.

Other stitches used, shown below in **bold italics,** are explained in the Techniques section.

See Plates 9 and 10 for practice pieces.

The lotus flower
Fig 1 shows the enlarged embroidery outline for the 8-petal Lotus, with the centre already worked. The method is also used for the 6-petal flower of the *Green pinwheel for Christmas.*

Petals and leaves – beading and edging
Petals and leaves, Figs 2 and 3, are worked in the same way, except for leaves with a beaded tip (Fig 4). Purl is stitched like a bead.

1. Lotus flower – working the centre
Double-stitch the central seed bead size 11°, as shown.
Back-stitch the eight surrounding beads, size 15°, Figs 1-3, p.82. Each should lie in a gap at the base between petal outlines. Take care not to pierce the thread of the previous stitch, as this will weaken it.

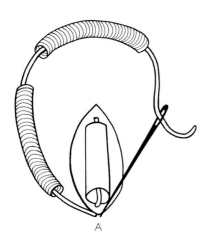

2. Beading a petal or leaf with a bugle bead and edging it with purl
Single-stitch the bugle bead. Cut two 5.5 mm (¼ in) lengths of purl. Bring up the needle at the base of the petal, at A. Thread on the two pieces of purl and take down the needle at A, forming a loop round the bugle bead.

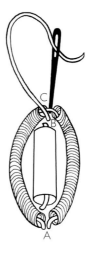

3. Securing the purl edging
Bring up the needle on the inside of the threaded purl, at B. Gently pull up the thread, positioning the pieces of purl on either side of the bugle bead. Pull the thread taut. Take down the needle, *over* the thread at C, as close to B as possible. Continue with the next petal.

Leaves with a beaded tip
These can be seen on the *Lotus thimble slipper* and
the *Lotus needle book*, and need extra care, Fig 4.

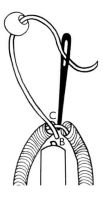

4. Sewing a bead at the tip of a leaf
Bring the needle up at B, thread on the bead and take the
needle down at C. Pull the thread gently to anchor the bead,
and the purl into its oval shape.

Couching a tight scroll
The basic method for **couching** stems has been
slightly modified for stems and tendrils with
tightly scrolled tips, Fig 1.

   Use a single strand of metallic cord or metallic
floss and work the couching stitches closer
together round the tight curves. This will allow
you to form well-rounded curves, despite the
small pattern outline.

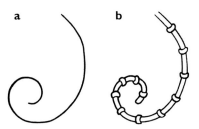

a   b

1. Stem or tendril with a tightly scrolled tip
a. Enlarged pattern outline

b. Tightly couched metallic cord
As the curve becomes tighter work the couching stitches
closer together, to obtain a well-rounded scroll. In addition,
where the curve is tightest make a few *knotting stitches* on
the back of the fabric. This will help keep the couched thread
in position and prevent loosening of the couching thread.

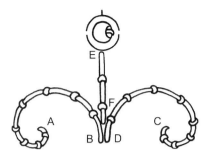

1. Tendrils and stems – couching metallic cord or floss

Work the tendrils and stems with a single length of metallic cord, **plunging** it (p.86) between the sections. At *B* and *D* **knot off** the couching thread but do not cut it off yet.

Starting at *A*, work in order of lettering. Bring up the cord at *A*, and the couching thread close by. Couch to *B*. Work the couching stitches closer together round the tight scroll, Fig 1b above. **Plunge** the cord at *B* and bring it up with the couching thread at *C*.

Couch from *C* to *D*. Plunge the cord at *D* and bring it up with the couching thread at *E*.

Couch from *E* to *F*. Plunge the cord at *F*, secure its ends (at *A* and *F*) with **whip stitches**, see Fig 4, p.86. Cut off the couching thread and the cord.

Bud sprigs – *Needle book* and *Bodkin holder* only
Work in the following stages:
- couch the tendrils and stems, Fig 1
- work the bud centre and its base (calyx), Fig 2
- bead the bud petals, Fig 3, and secure the purl tip, Fig 4
- ***double-stitch*** a single bead at the base of each stem and ***single-stitch*** a bead in each tendril coil.

Start at *A* and follow the order of lettering to *F*. The larger steps, from *B* to *C* and *D* to *E*, are designed to limit fastening off and damage to the silk. See also the *Guide to beading* in the project.

Small purl stitch
This simulates the pointed tip of the bud, Fig 4.

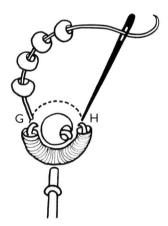

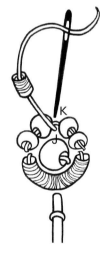

2. The bud – working the centre and base

Double-stitch the bead in the position shown.

Cut a 4 mm (less than ¼ in) length of purl. Bring the needle up at *G*, thread on the purl and take down the needle at *H*. Tension the thread so that the purl forms a curve round the bead.

3. The bud – beading the tight petals

Bring up the needle very close to *G*. Thread on four beads and take down the needle close to *H* to form a curve round the centre bead.

4. The bud – working the purl tip

Cut a length of purl, about 1 mm (¹⁄₁₆ in) long. Bring up the needle between the 2nd and 3rd bead, at *J*. Thread on the purl and take down the needle at *K*. Gently pull the thread taut and tie it off on the back of the fabric with a **knotting stitch**.

4 *Gifts & keepsakes*

Greetings card
Green pin wheel for Christmas
Key fob
Beaded tassels

Greetings card

Designed and worked by the author

This simpler project includes a five-petal flower surrounded by a floral border. The design also lends itself well to projects like the Small pouch with flower, shown here, and the miniature needle book and 'footstool' pin cushion on the cover. See Pl 10 for practice piece.

You will need

Embroidery hoop 15 cm (6 in), tracing paper and HB pencil, tissue paper and white dressmaker's carbon paper, embroidery needles sizes 8 and 12, and short beading needles size 12.

Fabric. Fine plain blue Indian silk, 25 cm (10 in) square. Same amount of iron-on fine interlining, e.g. vilene sofline or pellon.

Threads. Silver metallic cord, silver 100% viscose thread; blue Nymo* beading thread gauge D, or polyester thread.

Beads. Seed beads: size 11°, iridescent purple; size 15°, pearl white, clear translucent.

Construction. See Making up – simple mounting and *greetings card.*

* Nymo beading threads are sold in the UK without reference numbers. They must be conditioned before use by thorough stretching, to make them pliable and maintain an even tension.

Stitches

Double-stitching a bead, single-stitching a bead, straight-stitching beads, couching metallic thread, threading and couching beads.

All stitches are shown in the Embroidery notes in **bold italics** and, together with *Starting and fastening off threads* and directions for *Making up* will be found in the Techniques section, or on specified pages and Figures. You may need to refer to them while working the project.

Embroidery notes

Trace the embroidery outline, Fig 1 (*on p.54*), taking care to follow closely the even spacing of the five petals round the centre of the flower. Transfer it onto silk, following the procedure on

Greetings card
Embroidered with seed beads and metallic thread on fine plain mid-blue Indian silk.

Border stem and *flower stalk* are in silver metallic cord couched with silver viscose thread. *Flower centres* on the border and on *main flower* are iridescent purple 11° seed beads. *Petals* are pearl white 15°. *Flat beaded edging* is iridescent purple 11° and clear translucent 15°. Actual size.

p.67. This includes mounting the silk onto the hoop, ready for embroidery.

FRONT

Work in the following stages:

- bead the **four-petal** flowers, then the border leaves
- **couch** the border stem
- **couch** the flower stalk in the middle
- **thread and couch** the leaves on the stalk
- work the five-petal flower

Four-petal flower and border leaves

1. Follow Fig 2. Make a **double knot** to secure the Nymo thread on the back of the fabric and start with a four-petal flower, p.80. **Double-stitch** an iridescent purple bead 11° for the centre, and **single-stitch** the four pearl white beads 15° for the petals.

2. Embroider the leaves by **straight-stitching** pairs of clear translucent beads 15°. Make the straight stitch long enough for the beads to lie snugly together. Allow a tiny gap between the bases of each pair of leaves so the metallic cord can be couched between them without displacing the beads, Figs 1 and 2, p.80.

3. **Couch** the cord along the border stem line. It is important to tidy the ends of metallic cord on the back of the fabric to avoid a tangle, see Fig 6, in *Couching threads*.

The five-petal centre flower

4. *Stalk and leaves.* Couch the cord down the stalk line. **Thread and couch** clear translucent 15° beads for the four leaves, securing them on a slight curve, see Fig 2.

5. *Flower head.* Follow Fig 3. Double-stitch an iridescent purple 11° bead in the centre. Single-stitch a ring of five pearl white 15° beads, spacing them evenly round the centre, with a small gap between them and the centre bead.

Complete the petals by straight-stitching five sets of two pearl white 15° beads adjacent to the first ring. Note the angles at which the beads are stitched to maintain uniform triangular groups.

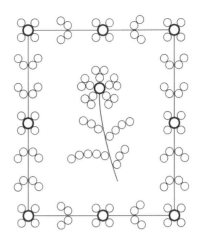

2. Guide to beading

Key

Lines – metallic cord
  straight and curved lines – border stem and flower stalk: single strand of silver metallic cord couched with silver viscose thread.

Circles – seed beads, sizes 11° and 15°
  heavier circles – flower centres: iridescent purple 11°.
  fine circles – petals, leaves: pearl white, clear translucent, 15°.

Work round the border beading the *four-petal flowers* and **straight-stitching** the leaves, Figs 1 and 2 p.80. **Couch** the border stem. Couch the flower stalk and **thread and couch** the leaves on a slight curve as shown. Work the five-petal flower, Fig 3.

3. Beading the five-petal flower

Double-stitch the purple 11° bead in the centre and **single-stitch** a ring of five white 15° beads around it, allowing a small gap round the centre bead. Finally **straight-stitch** five sets of two white 15° beads around the first ring, following the bead angles illustrated.

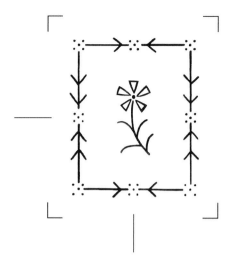

6. Remove the embroidery from the hoop, but don't cut it out yet.

7. For construction see *Making up*: *Simple mounting* and *Making up a card*. For the **flat beaded edging** see *Edging*s.

1. Embroidery outline for greetings card
Straight lines indicate the border stem, with its short leaves; the curved lines along the flower stalk are also leaves. Dots are flower centres and petals; the five triangles are the main flower petals.

Carefully trace the outline, the locating lines and corner marks, see *Preparing to embroider*. Actual size.

Pl 4. Small pouch with flower
Embroidered with seed beads sizes 11° and 15°, and stranded embroidery cotton on purple silk. The stem is in stem stitch, the flower centre bead is deep red, 11°, the petals pearl pink, 15°. Leaves are green translucent, 15°. Green, and pink silver-lined 15° beads are used for the flat beaded edging at top and bottom. The pouch is lined with pink silk and tied with a 3 mm (⅛ in) silk ribbon. Actual size.

Green pin wheel for Christmas

Designed and worked by the author

The design was inspired by a 19th century carved ivory pin wheel. With its star-like flower motif and ring of flowers symbolising the 12 days of Christmas, it makes a popular gift or decoration. The project is suitable for more experienced embroiderers. See Pl 9 for practice piece.

You will need

Embroidery hoop 15 cm (6 in), tracing paper and HB pencil, tissue paper and white dressmaker's carbon paper. Short beading needles size 12, embroidery needles sizes 8 and 12.

Fabric. Fine plain green Indian silk, 25 cm (10 in) square. Same amount of iron-on interlining, e.g. vilene softline or pellon.

Threads. White Nymo* beading thread gauge D; silver metallic cord**, silver 100% viscose thread; smooth silver metallic purl (gimp or bullion) size 9.

Beads. Seed beads: size 11°, metallic red; size 15°, pearl white. Bugle beads: 3 mm (⅛ in), bronzed maroon.

Construction. See *Making up – pin wheels.*

* Nymo beading threads are sold in the UK without reference numbers. They must be conditioned before use by thorough stretching, to make them pliable and maintain an even tension.

** Metallic thread, especially purl, will blunt sharp scissors. You can cut purl thread with a craft knife on a small felt-covered board.

Pin wheel for Christmas

Embroidered with seed beads, bugle beads, smooth metallic purl and metallic cord on fine plain green Indian silk. The back has different bead colours.

The *floral star motif* has a centre of metallic red seed beads, 11°. The six *petals* are 3 mm (⅛ in) bronzed maroon bugle beads, edged with silver purl and a pearl white seed bead, 15°, at the tip. *Stamens* are couched single strands of silver cord, tipped with metallic red seed beads, 11°.

Twelve *flower heads* are embroidered with a metallic red seed bead, 11° at the centre, ringed by eight pearl white seed beads, 15°. Actual size.

Stitches

Beading 6- to 8-petal flowers, edging with purl, couching metallic thread, double-stitching beads, threading and couching beads.

All stitches and techniques are shown in the Embroidery notes in **bold italics** and, together with *Starting and fastening off threads* and directions for *Making up* will be found in the Techniques section, or on specified pages and Figures. You may need to refer to them while working the project.

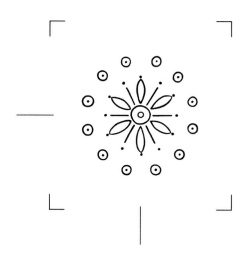

1. Embroidery outline for green pin wheel

The centre of the floral star is a small circle surrounded by a larger circle representing the inner ring of small petals. Pointed ovals with dots at their tips show the main petals. Straight lines with a dot show the stamens and their tips. Dotted circles round the edge represent the small eight-petal flowers.

Tracing and transferring the outline needs to be done carefully to maintain the symmetry of the design: take care over the curved lines of the petals, and make sure the stamen tips, as well as the ring of twelve flowers, are set in a circle and equally spaced.

Trace the outline and locating lines, see *Preparing to embroider*. Actual size.

Embroidery notes

Trace the embroidery outline, Fig 1, and transfer it and the pattern parts on to the silk, following the procedure on p.67. This includes mounting the silk on to the hoop, ready for embroidery.

Tracing and transferring the embroidery outline, especially the curved outlines and the spacing between the single beads, should be done carefully to maintain the symmetry of the design.

FRONT

Work in the following stages:
* embroider the floral star motif in the centre
* work the ring of flowers round the edge

Star motif
1. *Centre*. Follow Fig 2 below, and Figs 1-3 on p.47. Use metallic red seed beads, all 11°. **Double-stitch** the central bead as shown, then **back-stitch** the six surrounding beads. Each should lie in a gap at the base between petal outlines.
2. *Petals*. Work the petals with six 3 mm (⅛ in) bronzed maroon bugle beads, setting them between the centre beads already in position. **Edge** them with purl, adding a pearl white 15° bead on each tip if you wish, Fig 4, p.48.
3. *Stamens*. **Couch** the metallic cord with viscose thread. It is important to tidy the ends of cord on the back of the fabric to avoid a tangle, see Fig 6, p.88.

Top each stamen with a metallic red bead, 11°, double-stitched. Sew them on a circle defined by the tips of the petals, as shown in Fig 2 and the photograph on p.55.

Outer ring of 12 flowers
4. Ensure the fabric is held taut in the hoop. Bead the flowers, p.81 using the quicker method: **double-stitch** a metallic red bead 11° at the centre then **thread and couch** eight pearl white 15° beads around it.

2. Guide to beading

Key

Lines – couched metallic thread

pointed ovals – petal outlines: smooth metallic purl, secured by a stitch

straight lines – stamens: couched metallic cord

Rectangles within ovals – bugle beads: bronzed maroon, 3 mm ($\frac{1}{8}$ in)

Circles – seed beads, sizes 11° and 15°

heavier circles – centre of star motif, centres of small flowers, stamen tips: metallic red, 11°

fine circles – tips of main petals, petals of outer ring of flowers: pearl white, 15°

Start with the centre. ***Double-stitch*** the centre bead and ***back-stitch*** the ring of six beads, p.47. Make sure the six beads are stitched between the bases of adjacent petals, as shown. Bead a petal with a bugle bead, ***edge*** it with purl, and ***single-stitch*** the bead to each tip, Figs 2–4, pp.47–48. Repeat for the remaining petals. ***Couch*** all the stamens in turn, then top each with a double-stitched bead. No need to cut off threads between stages.

   Embroider the twelve flowers round the edge, p.81.

BACK

The position of the Back should already have been outlined on the silk. If you plan to bead the Back, proceed to 5. Otherwise go to 7. but don't cut out either pattern part yet.

5. To embroider the Back, remove the silk from the hoop. Transfer the embroidery outline, Fig 1, on to the silk as before, then mount the silk back on to the hoop.

6. Work the Back using the same techniques as for the Front, and bead in contrasting colours if you wish.

7. Remove the embroidery from the hoop. For construction, see *Making up*.

Key fob or scissors keep

Designed and worked by Helen Payne

This design is an adaptation of the centre of the Victorian needle book, made to hang from the key of an old sewing box. It also makes a charming pendant or, with a longer cord, a scissors keep. The same design can be embroidered on the Back.

You will need

Embroidery hoop 15 cm (6 in), tracing paper and HB pencil, tissue paper and blue dressmaker's carbon paper. Embroidery needles sizes 8 and 12; short beading needle size 12.

Fabric. Fine plain yellow Indian silk, 25 cm (10 in) square. Same amount of iron-on fine interlining, e.g. vilene softline or pellon.

Threads. Two strands of gold metallic embroidery floss, 100% gold viscose thread; cream Nymo* beading thread gauge D, or light gold polyester thread.

Beads. Seed beads, size 15°; translucent gold-lined, cobalt blue silver-lined.

Construction. See *Making up – key fob.*

* Nymo beading threads are sold in the UK without reference numbers. They must be conditioned before use by thorough stretching, to make them pliable and maintain an even tension.

Stitches

Beading 6- to 8-petal flowers, couching metallic thread, straight-stitching beads.

All stitches and techniques are shown in the Embroidery notes in **bold italics** and, together with *Starting and fastening off threads* and directions for *Making up* will be found in the Techniques section, or on specified pages and Figures. You may need to refer to them while working the project.

Embroidery notes

Trace the embroidery outline, Fig 1, and transfer it and the pattern parts on to the silk, following the procedure on p.67. This includes mounting the silk on to the hoop, ready for embroidery.

Key fob

Embroidered with seed beads, all size 15°, and gold metallic embroidery floss on fine plain yellow Indian silk.

Stems in gold metallic floss. *Flower centres* and *leaves* in translucent gold-lined beads; *petals* in cobalt blue, silver-lined. *Picot edging* in the same two colours. *Twisted cord* and *simple tassel* in light old gold thread. Actual size.

58

FRONT

Work in the following stages:
- bead the flower in the centre
- *couch* the longer stems, then the shorter ones
- work the remaining flowers
- *straight-stitch* the leaves

Flowers and stems

1. Follow Fig 2 and Pl 5. First bead the flower marked *, p.82. **Double-stitch** a translucent gold-lined bead for the centre and **back-stitch** 8 cobalt blue silver-lined beads around it for the petals (as used here) or try the Quicker method, p.81.

2. *Stems.* Start at the upper left and **couch** two strands of gold metallic floss with gold viscose thread along the stem lines. Plunge the threads behind the worked central flower and bring them up just in front. Continue towards the lower right tip and plunge the threads to the back of the fabric. It is important to tidy the ends of metallic floss on the back of the fabric to avoid a tangle, see Fig 6, p.88. Work the other diagonal stem, starting from the top right, then the shorter stems.

3. Bead the remaining flowers.

Leaves

4. Leaves are shown on the pattern by short lines. **Straight stitch** a pair of translucent gold-lined beads for each leaf.

BACK

5. The position of the Back should already have been outlined on the silk. If you plan to embroider the Back, proceed to *6*; otherwise go to *8*. but don't cut out either pattern part yet.

6. To embroider the Back, remove the silk from the hoop. Transfer the embroidery outline, Fig 1, on to the silk once more, then mount the silk on to the hoop.

7. Work the Back using the same method as for the Front, and bead in contrasting colours if you wish.

8. Remove the embroidery from the hoop. For construction see *Making up*, for **picot edging** and **twisted cord** see *Edgings*.

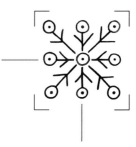

1. Embroidery outline for key fob
Lines show the stems, and their short offshoots are leaves; the circles are flowers.

Carefully trace the outline, the locating lines and corner marks, see *Preparing to embroider*. Actual size.

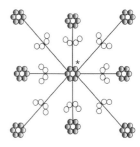

2. Guide to beading
Key
Lines – stems: two adjacent strands of metallic embroidery floss couched with viscose thread.
Circles – seed beads, all size 15°
  plain circles – centres of flowers, and leaves: translucent gold-lined.
  filled circles – rings of petals: 8 cobalt blue silver-lined.
First bead the flower marked *, p.82. Then, starting from top left, **couch** the diagonal stems, plunging the threads behind the worked centre flower and bringing them up again just in front, p.86. Couch the remaining stems. Bead the remaining flowers. **Straight stitch** pairs of beads for the leaves.

Pl 5. Centre of key fob. Enlarged.

Beaded tassel

Designed and worked by the author

This unusual beaded tassel is made from the frayed selvedge of silk fabric rather than conventionally from thread. It makes an attractive decoration attached to a key or embroidery scissors, or on dress, and a very acceptable gift. Try using shot silk for exciting colour effects.

Beaded tassels
The tassels are made from silk fabric. The tassel head is the unfrayed selvedge strip. Warp threads are frayed away, so that the remaining weft threads form the fringe. The selvedge strip is rolled and beaded to form the head, which has a loop of twisted cord at the top. Enlarged.

You will need

A fine embroidery needle, a short beading needle, sharps or appliqué size 12, a fine pin, small sharp scissors; PVA fabric adhesive, a cotton wool bud.
Fabric. Plain or shot Indian silk, 80 × 35 mm (3 × 1 ¼ in), cut along the selvedge.
Threads. 100% viscose, or fine silk thread matching the fabric; Nymo* beading thread gauge D, or polyester thread, matching the fabric. Three strands of silk embroidery thread for the twisted cord.
Beads. Seed beads size 15°.

* Nymo beading threads are sold in the UK without reference numbers. They must be conditioned before use by thorough stretching, to make them pliable and maintain an even tension.

Stitches

Making twisted cord, oversewing, stab stitch, beaded blanket stitch.

Stitches used only in this design are explained in the Embroidery notes and diagrams and shown in **bold** type. Techniques shown in ***bold italics*** are used in other projects and will be found in the Techniques section.

Embroidery notes

1. Starting from the middle of the long raw edge, fray the fabric by carefully drawing away one or two threads at a time with the tip of a fine needle. Fray up to the selvedge strip, which will form the tassel head and should be one third of the tassel length.
2. Make a ***twisted cord*** with three strands of silk thread, 150 mm (6 in) long. Using viscose thread bind the end of the twisted cord and secure it with several stitches right through the strands near the knot. The cord can then be cut off without untwisting. Cut off the knot.
3. Fold and glue the short raw edges of the fabric, Fig 1.
4. ***Oversew*** the ends of the cord to the folded ends of the fabric. Ensure the cord covers the whole width of the selvedge strip, as shown in Fig 2.

5. Bring the folded edges together and join them with oversewing. This will form a firm core for the tassel. Roll up the selvedge, Fig 3, and secure the roll temporarily with a pin, Fig 4.

6. Secure the upper edge of the roll with several small stitches stabbed through the layers and start beading the lower edge with **beaded blanket stitches**, Figs 5-7.

7. Trim the tassel, Fig 8.

1. Gluing the short edges
Place the frayed fabric on a solid surface. Apply adhesive *sparingly* with a cotton bud to one short edge. Fold it into a narrow hem about 3 mm (⅛ in) wide and press between your fingers until set. Repeat for the other short edge.

2. Attaching the twisted cord to the fabric
Oversew the ends of the cord down the whole of each hemmed edge leaving a loop above.

3. Forming the rolled tassel head
Fold the fabric in two and oversew the edges together to form the tassel core.

Holding the *stitched* edge firmly between thumb and forefinger, roll the fabric *tightly* round the core. Make sure the entire top edge of the roll is level.

4. Securing the head
Secure the roll temporarily with a fine pin, then oversew down the folded edge. Remove the pin. Make several small *stab stitches* through the top edge of the roll, to keep the top level during beading.

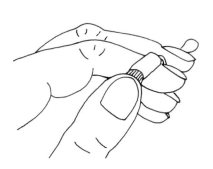

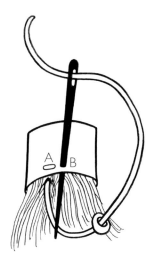

5. Preparing to bead

Hold the fringe and cord of the tassel between thumb and forefinger, with the cord tucked underneath the middle finger. The tassel head will lie over the index finger ready for beading.

6. Beading the tassel head with *blanket-stitch* (enlarged)

Insert a thread with a knotted end inside an inner layer and draw it to the surface. Make a small stitch, A, take the thread down below the surface and bring it up again through the fringe, as shown. Working from left to right, thread a bead and insert the needle vertically at B, through 2 or 3 layers of fabric. Bring the needle up below B, through the edge of the fringe and over the loop, as shown. Pull the thread taut to secure the first bead.

Continue beading round the lower edge of the tassel head and repeat at the top edge. Match the length of stitch to the width of the beads so they lie snugly round the tassel.

7. Completed tassel head

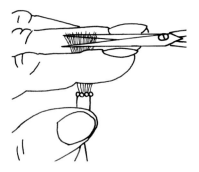

8. Finishing

Trim the edge of the fringe with a pair of sharp scissors as shown.

Techniques

*This section provides comprehensive support for the embroiderer working or making up the projects. It explains in detail the stitches highlighted in **bold** italics in the projects. Some small practice pieces are included.*

Tools and materials

This section provides general information on tools and materials used throughout the book. They are listed broadly in the order they are required.

Tools and materials required for embroidery are listed at the start of each project. Those needed for construction are listed at the start of each Making up section.

You will probably already own some of these tools and materials, like a hoop frame and embroidery scissors. Others are available from haberdashery or craft supply shops, see also Suppliers.

Hoop frames An embroidery hoop is essential for stretching the fabric in all the projects, except the starter project and the tassel. The stretching enables you to tension the stitches correctly, both for beading and for couching. Use either a 15 cm (6 in) or an 18 cm (7 in) hoop frame. Before starting, bind the inner hoop tightly all the way round with cotton tape.

The use of a larger hoop frame saves ironing the fabric before starting to make up the accessory.

Tracing paper and HB pencil for tracing the pattern outline. Ensure the pencil is sharp and the paper of good quality.

Fine-tipped spent ball-point pen or HB pencil for transferring the embroidery outline on to silk.

A sharp white or silver pencil can be useful for emphasizing the outline of the pattern on a darker silk, Pl 7, p.75.

White tissue paper for transferring pattern layouts on to the silk.

Dressmaker's carbon paper for transferring embroidery outlines. Use a colour to contrast with your silk, e.g. white for a blue silk, Pl 7, p.75.

Needles and pins
Beading needles. Short or appliqué needles, size 12, can be used for all projects.

Needles for metallic threads. The eye of the needle must be large enough to carry the thread through the fabric without damaging the outer layer of the metallic thread.

For floss use a size 8 embroidery needle; for cord a size 5 or 3 quilting needle. Smaller needles can damage the thread. Purl (gimp or bullion) is stitched like a bead, so use a beading needle.
Needles for couching with viscose thread. Use size 12 embroidery or appliqué needles.
Needles for embroidering with silk thread. Use size 12 embroidery needles and a single strand of silk.
Fine pins. Often sold as 'lace' or 'silk' pins. Stainless steel are best. Dressmaker's pins are too thick for the fine fabric.

Scissors
Embroidery scissors. These have fine thin pointed blades and are used for cutting viscose, Nymo and silk threads, fine fabrics and vilene. A small pair of general purpose scissors can be used to cut metallic threads and purl, which can blunt embroidery scissors. Metallic purl (gimp or bullion) can also be cut with a craft knife (e.g. Stanley knife) on a felt-covered board.
Scissors for cutting Dutch grey board (thick card, found as backing on memo pads). General purpose sharp scissors about 12.5 cm (5 in) long, or 'craft scissors', are suitable.

A magnifier helps in working the embroidery and beading of small projects. Watchmakers' magnifiers worn round the head and clip-on types for glasses are among the devices available, and an important aid, see *Suppliers*.

Fabrics and linings
Fabrics Fine plain smooth Indian silk is used for most projects, but soft denim or calico can be used for the *Starter project* and *Practice pieces*.

continued overleaf

Pl 6. Materials for bead embroidery ▶
Beading needles, metallic cord, seed beads, bugle beads and metallic purl (gimp or bullion).

Smaller projects can be made from silk smaller than specified by adding temporary calico strips around the edges before stretching in the hoop.
Interlining Vilene 308 white, lightweight ultrasoft iron-on, is used for lining the silk before transferring the embroidery pattern. Pellon 906F is an alternative available in USA and Canada.
Padding Vilene 240 white, extra heavy sew-in. This interlining material is used to pad Dutch grey board in the making up stage. Pellon 70W is available in USA and Canada, but is thicker than Vilene 240. If used for padding the grey board during making up, cut the fabric 1 mm beyond the tacked outline to increase overlap.

Polyester felt 1 to 2 mm (about $\frac{1}{16}$ in) thick, available from patchwork and quilting suppliers, is used to pad the mounting board for the *Needle books* and the *Periwinkle*. Pellon 989 Quilter's fleece is an alternative available in USA and Canada.
Needle pages Use fine woollen fabric or fine felt.

Threads

Metallic threads

In this book single (thicker) metallic threads are termed 'cord' to differentiate them from the stranded metallic floss. Both comprise metallic material coiled round a core and are marked on couching diagrams with fine diagonal lines.
Metallic cord is a single thread, roughly equivalent to two strands of floss. Madeira Metallic Nos 6 and 12, on reels, are suitable; No 12 is more pliable.
Stranded metallic embroidery floss, e.g. from DMC, is used double-stranded and is more pliable than cord. Try to couch the two strands side by side, rather than twisted around each other.
Metallic purl, also known as gimp or bullion. Although thread-like in appearance, this is a coil and is stitched like a bead. Purl size 9 is used for the *Beaded lotus* projects and for the *Green pin wheel for Christmas*. Avoid stretching as it is not springy.
Viscose (100%) embroidery thread (e.g. Güttermann) is used to couch metallic threads.
Nymo thread (medium, or gauge D) comes in

several colours and is used for stitching beads in all projects, and for metallic purl. It needs to be conditioned before use by thorough stretching to make it pliable.
Silk Stranded embroidery silk is used for making the twisted cords, and silk embroidery floss for the leaves on the *Pin basket*.
Coton perlé is a smooth cotton thread used for the twisted cord of the *Starter project*, and for the couching *Practice piece*.

Beads (see Pl 6)
Seed beads, sizes 11° and 15°, are used in most of the projects. Size 15° beads, the smallest, are sometimes called 'petite'.
Bugle beads, size 3 mm, are used for the *Beaded lotus* projects and the *Green pin wheel for Christmas*.

Beading mat of material with a short dense pile, approximately 35×30 cm (14×12 in). An indispensable bead-retaining work surface!

Cutting board
A plastic 'self-healing' surface with a grid which allows repeated cutting with a sharp knife.

Dutch grey board (unlined)
Normally used as backing of memo pads (thick card). A weight of 445 gsm (750 microns) was used for mounting the panels of most projects.

Mounting board
Used by picture framers, a convenient source of off-cuts. Used for mounting the *Needle book*, *Periwinkle* and *Greetings card* projects.

Adhesive
PVA, a white opaque liquid glue used to attach fabric to board or card.

Preparing to embroider

Tracing and transferring the outlines

For the projects, work in the following stages:
• Trace the embroidery outline
• Prepare the fabric
• Position the pattern outlines
• Transfer the embroidery outline on to the fabric

Projects

Tracing the embroidery outline
1. Trace the embroidery outline, including the two locating lines and corner markings (where shown), on to quality tracing paper using a sharp HB pencil. Accuracy is important. Alternatively, photocopy the outline directly on to tracing paper. Make only one tracing: even if the project has two sides, each will be worked in turn from the same tracing. Set aside the tracing.

Preparing the fabric
2. Cut the silk fabric and the iron-on interlining to size, as specified in your project. Allow at least 5 cm (2 in) outside the hoop for stretching. It helps if one edge is a selvedge, or is frayed to give a straight edge.
3. Iron the silk if necessary. Place the silk over the interlining and press on with a dry iron set to 'silk'.

Positioning the pattern outlines
4. Select the layout guide for your project from Figs 1-11. Cut a piece of tissue paper to the size of the silk. Trace the *broken* outlines of the pattern parts, *including* the two locating lines and the straight grain line.
5. Fold the tissue paper back on top along the traced straight grain line and align the folded edge with the straight grain of the silk. Pin one left-hand corner of the tissue paper to the silk. Pin the other three corners while carefully straightening out the tissue paper.

Practice pieces

For *Practice pieces* follow this simpler procedure:
1. *Tracing the embroidery outline*. Trace the embroidery outline on to quality tracing paper using a sharp HB pencil. Accuracy is important. Alternatively, photocopy the outline directly on to tracing paper.
2. *Transferring the outline onto fabric*. Iron the fabric if necessary. Position the tracing in the middle of the fabric. Pin it as shown in Fig 10, but ignore the locating lines and corner marks. Insert a piece of dressmaker's carbon paper, *face down*, between the tracing and the fabric. Trace the pattern with a sharp HB pencil; press hard. Remove the upper right pin and the carbon paper. Check the transfer is complete. If not, reinsert the carbon paper, re-pin and re-trace the missing part.
3. Mount the fabric on the hoop. You are now ready to embroider.

6. With a fine thread tack the *broken* outlines and the two locating lines on to the silk, Pl 7. Gently score the tissue paper close to the tacked lines with the tip of a needle, then carefully tear away the tissue paper

continued on p.73

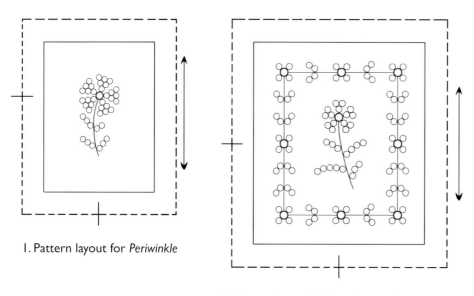

1. Pattern layout for *Periwinkle*

2. Pattern layout for *Greetings card*

1. & 2. Single panels – pattern layouts

These notes cover the *Periwinkle* and the *Greetings card*.

The solid outlines define the edges of the mounting board. Arrows indicate the straight grain. The broken outlines show the edges of the pattern parts, and the two short marks are locating lines.

Trace the broken outlines and locating lines on to tissue paper and tack them on to the silk. Actual size.

3. Pin cushion with floral border – pattern layout

The solid outlines on Front and Back define the edges of the piece. Arrows indicate the straight grain. The broken outlines show the edges of the pattern parts, and the two short marks are locating lines.

Trace the broken outlines and locating lines on to tissue paper and tack them on to the silk. Actual size.

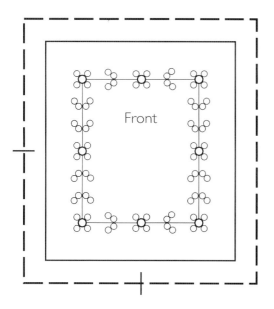

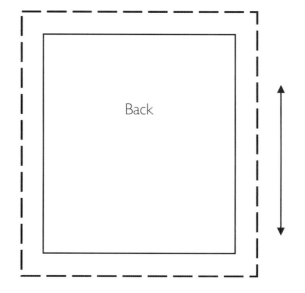

4. Key fob or scissors keep – pattern layout

The solid outlines on Front and Back define the edges of the board. Arrows indicate the straight grain. The broken outlines show the edges of the pattern parts, and the two short marks are locating lines.

Trace the broken outlines and locating lines on to tissue paper and tack them on to the silk. Actual size.

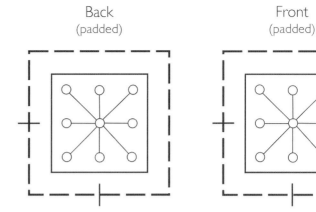

Back (padded)   Front (padded)

5. Pin wheels – pattern layout

The solid outlines on Front and Back define the edges of the board. Arrows indicate the straight grain. The broken outlines show the edges of the pattern parts, and the two short marks are locating lines.

Trace the broken outlines and locating lines on to tissue paper and tack them on to the silk. Actual size.

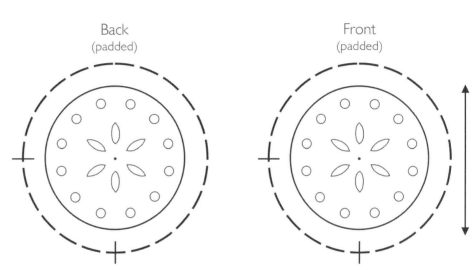

Back (padded)   Front (padded)

6. Pin basket – pattern layout

The solid outlines on Front and Back define the edges of the board. Arrows indicate the straight grain. The broken outlines show the edges of the pattern parts, and the two short marks are locating lines.

Trace the broken outlines and locating lines on to tissue paper and tack them on to the silk. Actual size.

Back (padded)   Front (padded)

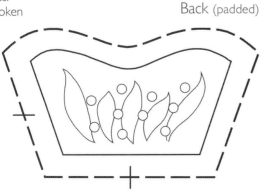
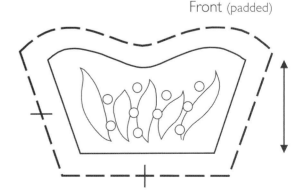

69

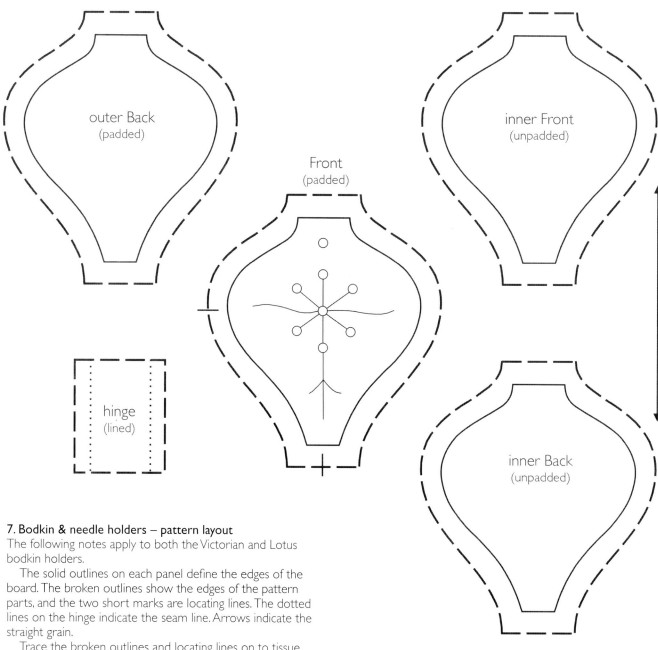

outer Back
(padded)

inner Front
(unpadded)

Front
(padded)

hinge
(lined)

inner Back
(unpadded)

7. Bodkin & needle holders – pattern layout

The following notes apply to both the Victorian and Lotus bodkin holders.

The solid outlines on each panel define the edges of the board. The broken outlines show the edges of the pattern parts, and the two short marks are locating lines. The dotted lines on the hinge indicate the seam line. Arrows indicate the straight grain.

Trace the broken outlines and locating lines on to tissue paper and tack them on to the silk. Actual size.

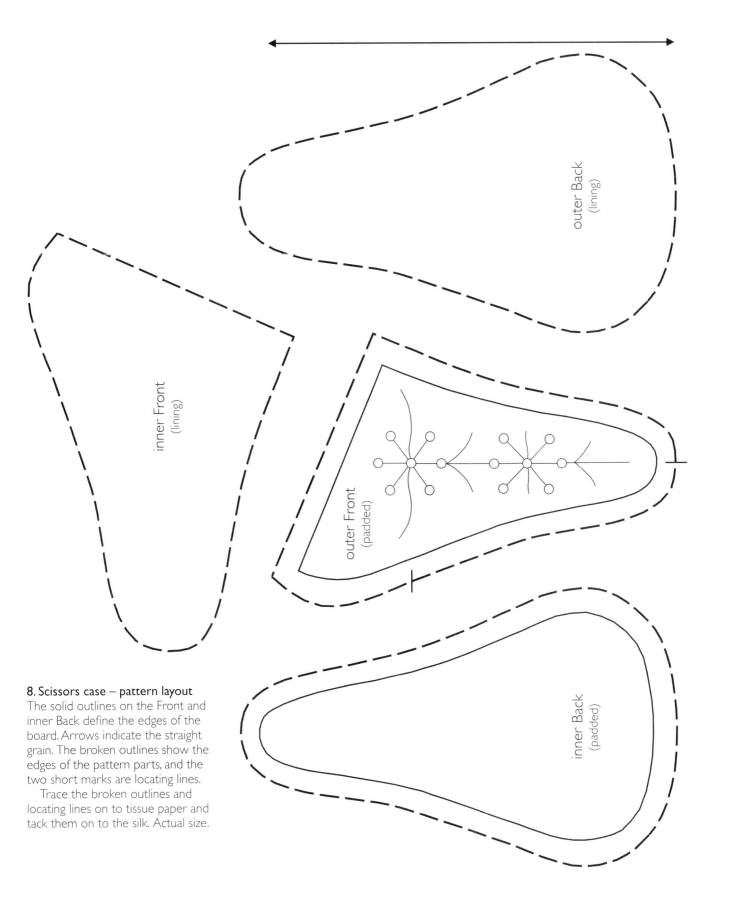

outer Back
(lining)

inner Front
(lining)

outer Front
(padded)

inner Back
(padded)

8. Scissors case – pattern layout
The solid outlines on the Front and
inner Back define the edges of the
board. Arrows indicate the straight
grain. The broken outlines show the
edges of the pattern parts, and the
two short marks are locating lines.
   Trace the broken outlines and
locating lines on to tissue paper and
tack them on to the silk. Actual size.

Transferring the embroidery outline on to silk

7. Position the traced embroidery outline over the area for beading by aligning its two locating lines with those already tacked on the silk. Pin the tracing in place on three corners, Fig 10.

For projects embroidered on two sides start with the Front. The Back should be transferred and worked only after the embroidery of the Front is completed.

8. Slip a piece of dressmaker's carbon paper *face down* between the tracing and the silk. For darker silk use light paper, and for lighter silk a dark one.

9. Transfer the design on to the silk by tracing with a sharp HB pencil or spent fine ball point pen, but *don't* transfer the locating lines or the corner markings (if present). Press hard to obtain a clear outline. *Don't* cut out any of the pattern parts at this stage.

10. Mount the silk on the hoop, wherever possible keeping the tacked outlines within the perimeter, Pl 7, p.75.

You are now ready to embroider.

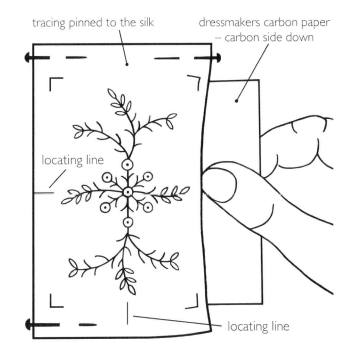

tracing pinned to the silk

dressmakers carbon paper – carbon side down

locating line

locating line

10. Transferring the embroidery outline on to the silk
Position and pin the tracing to the silk as directed in 7. above. Insert a piece of dressmaker's carbon paper, *face down*, between the tracing and the silk. Trace the pattern with a sharp HB pencil; press hard. Do not trace the corner marks or the locating lines. Remove the upper right pin and the carbon paper. Check the transfer is complete. If not, reinsert the carbon paper, re-pin and re-trace the missing part.

◀

9. Needle books – pattern layouts
a. Victorian needle book
b. Lotus needle book
The following notes apply to both the Victorian and Lotus needle books, though the Lotus version is slightly larger.

The solid outlines on Front and Back define the edges of the board; on the Spine they define the pattern for the lining strip. Arrows indicate the straight grain. The broken outlines show the edges of the pattern parts, and the two short marks are locating lines.

Trace the broken outlines and locating lines on to tissue paper and tack them on to the silk. Actual size.

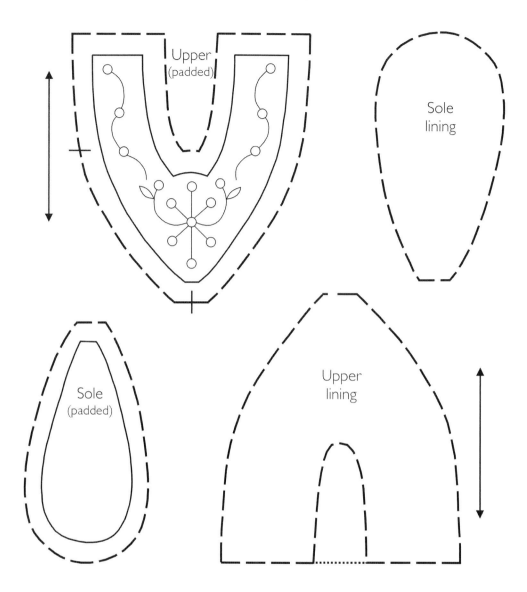

11. Thimble slippers – pattern layout

The following notes apply to both the Victorian and Lotus thimble slippers.

The solid outlines on the Upper and the Sole define the edges of the board. The dotted line on the Upper lining pattern defines the inner area which should be left uncut until the outer edge has been pinned to the board, Pl 18. Arrows indicate the straight grain. The broken outlines show the edges of the pattern parts, and the two short marks are locating lines.

Trace the broken outlines and locating lines on to tissue paped and tack them on to the silk, Pl 7 opposite. Actual size.

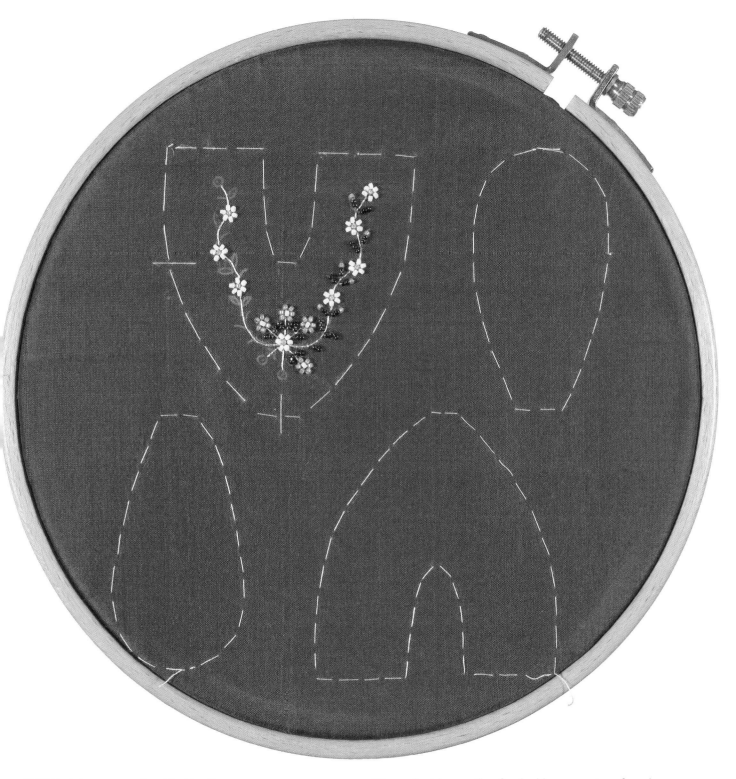

Pl 7. Work in progress for thimble slipper
Outlines of pattern parts tacked on to silk stretched in a 15 cm (6 in) hoop.

The embroidery outline for the Upper was transferred on to the silk using pale dressmaker's carbon paper. It was centred over the tacked outline, and aligned with the straight grain using the short locating lines.

Starting and fastening off threads

Both stitches are worked on the back of the fabric.

Knotted back stitch for starting
The knotted back stitch is used to anchor a couching or beading thread. The needle is taken through the loop of a back stitch.

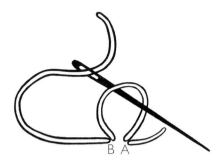

1. Knotted back stitch
Work on the back of the fabric, as shown.

Make a straight stitch from A to B, leaving a short tail of thread on the surface. Take down the needle again at A and up at B leaving a loop. Thread the needle through the loop and pull the thread taut to form a knot. Trim the tail of the thread.

Knotting stitch for fastening off and tensioning
This stitch is used to fasten off, or to maintain tension in a couching thread. It is worked on the back of the fabric.

1. *To fasten off.* Make one stitch to fasten off a beading thread; make two successive stitches to fasten off a couching thread.

When working between parts of a design up to about 3 mm (⅛ in) apart you can fasten off the thread, but need not cut it off between each part. For greater distances the thread should be fastened off *and* cut off, and the process restarted with a knotted back stitch.

2. *Maintaining tension round tight scrolls.* Make several knotting stitches close together to maintain tension and prevent loosening of the couching thread.

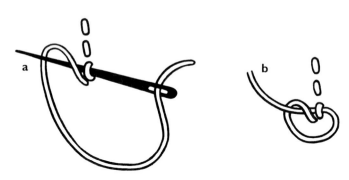

2. Working a knotting stitch
Work on the back of the fabric, as shown.

a. Thread the needle through the last stitch but *not* through the fabric. Make a loop round the end of the needle.

b. Pull the thread through to form a loose knot, then tighten it. Repeat on the stitch above the last and cut off the thread.

For tight scrolls work the knotting stitches close together to maintain tension in the couching thread.

Beading stitches

Stitches are listed roughly in the order they appear in the book.

All beading stitches used are listed below. Those common to several projects (highlighted in the projects by **bold italics**) are explained here in detail. Stitches used only in the *Beaded lotus* or single projects (highlighted there in **bold**), are listed here but explained where they are used. For starting and fastening off threads see opposite.

- An embroidery hoop is essential. Bead embroidery requires the needle to pass *vertically up and down* through a stretched fabric, which can only be achieved on a hoop.
- Your work will look best if you can keep the beads firmly upright. So it is important to match the length of stitch to the bead hole, see *Single-stitching* below.
- Try practising beading stitches on a spare piece of calico or fine cotton before starting to bead on silk. Or try one of the three *Practice pieces*, pp.80, 83, 87.

BASIC TECHNIQUES
Single-stitching a bead
Examples of single-stitched beads are: petals in the four-petal flowers on the floral border of the *Pin cushion*; the first bead in a row or circle of back-stitched beads and the tips of buds seen in the Victorian style projects.

The length of stitch is important in making the bead sit well on the silk: it should match the length of the bead hole, *A-B* on Fig 1. Beginners should practise sewing a bead singly before starting a project.

Double-stitching a bead
This stitch is used where a bead is a single or central feature of a design to anchor it firmly to the silk, as in flower centres.

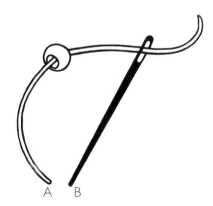

1. Single-stitching a bead
Bring up the needle at *A*, thread on a single bead and take the needle down at *B*. Make the distance *A-B* equal to the length of the bead hole, so the bead is held upright on the silk without exposing extra thread. Pull the thread taut.

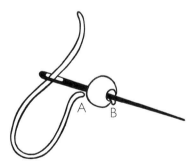

2. Double-stitching a bead
Complete the single stitch, Fig 1. Bring up the needle again at *A*, thread it through the bead, take down the needle at *B* and pull the thread through. If the bead is a single feature, *knot off* the thread (at the back of the work).

Straight-stitching a line of beads

This stitch is quick to work and used for small straight leaves, as in the *Pin cushion* and the *Greetings card* flower, also for triangular petals in the *Periwinkle*, see *Practice piece*, Pl 8, p.80. A line of beads, no more than four at a time, is threaded and secured with a single stitch. It allows the beads to lie close together. Ensure that the silk in the hoop is stretched taut and use a fine or medium beading thread.

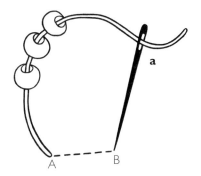

1. Working a straight stitch
a. Bring up the needle at *A*, thread on the beads required to fill the space, lay them close together along the outline and check they fit before taking down the needle at *B*. Pull the thread taut.
b. The completed straight stitch.

Threading and couching beads

This is a straightforward technique following on from straight-stitching. It is used for the straight lines on Victorian style leaves and buds, Figs 1 and 2; and for the curved lines on leaves of the *Periwinkle*, Figs 3 and 4.

Threading and couching along a straight line

1. Threading the beads
The line *A-B* shows the space to be beaded. Bring up the needle at *A*. Thread on enough beads to fill the space loosely. Here three beads are sufficient. Take the needle down at *B*.

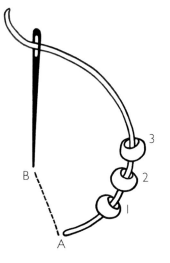

2. The couching stitches
Bring up the needle at *C*, between the end and middle beads. Take down the thread at *D*, making sure the thread forms a stitch over the beading thread. Pull the thread through to complete the first couching stitch, *C-D*. Bring up the needle at *E* and take it down at *F* to form a further couching stitch between the two lower beads.

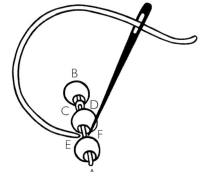

Threading and couching round a curve

To assess the number of beads required: push the threaded beads down to the base of the thread with your thumb and forefinger, laying them temporarily along the curved stitching line. Fewer, rather than more beads, will lie better!

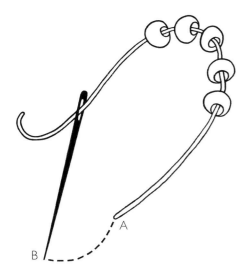

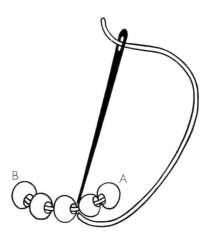

3. Threading the beads

Bring up the needle at one end of the curved line, *A*. Thread on enough beads to loosely fill the required space. Take down the needle at *B*. Pull the thread through *loosely* to follow the curve.

4. Couching the beads

First anchor the thread near the centre of the curve with a couching stitch, gently pulling the core thread with the tip of the needle so the beads follow the curve. Working out from the centre, couch between the other beads similarly.

Back-stitching beads on a curve

This technique is used in several projects and mainly for the rings of petals in Victorian style flowers, see *Flowers with a ring of 6-8 petals* below.

1. Back-stitching beads

The curved embroidery outline is shown by a broken line.
  Single-stitch the first bead from *A* to *B*, as shown. Subsequent beads will be sewn backwards (*back-stitched*), towards the previous bead. Bring up the needle at *C*, thread on the second bead and take down the needle at *B*. Match the length of the stitch to the length of the bead hole. Continue back-stitching the remaining beads along the outline.

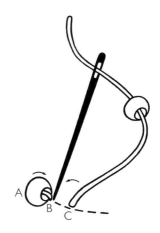

BEADING FLOWERS

A surprising range of flowers can be created from just a limited choice of beads and a variety of stitches.

Four-petal flowers

These tiny stylised flowers are features of the *Pin cushion* and the *Flower card*. Selecting a colour for the larger centre bead which contrasts with the petals colour is particularly effective. A single flower worked at the top of a curved stalk also makes an attractive motif.

The four-petal flower is marked on embroidery outlines by five dots, and on beading guides by five circles.

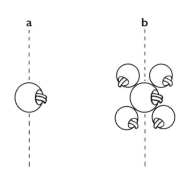

1. Working the flower
a. Secure the large bead in the centre with a **double stitch**, with the hole at right angles to the stem outline.
b. *Single-stitch* the four beads in turn, spacing them equally round the centre bead. Note the angles of the stitches.

2. Spacing between leaves
Note the gap between the leaves which allows space for *couching* the metallic cord.

Flowers with five triangular petals

Triangular petals formed with either three or six beads can be seen in the *Greetings card*, *Small pouch with flower*, and *Periwinkle* projects.

Sets of **straight-stitched** beads are added to a centre to form larger triangular petals, see Pl 8. Special care is required when positioning the stitches on the second or third row to maintain the triangular shape.

Embroidery outline

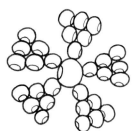

Guide to beading
Note the positioning of the beads

Flowers with a ring of 6 to 8 petals

The embroidery outline shows the flowers as a circle with a centre dot. They can be worked by a Quicker or Standard method, but the Standard method gives a more realistic look by spacing the petals. A *Practice piece* with larger beads using the Standard method is shown in Pl 9, p.83.

Always bead any flowers marked * first.

Quicker method – *threading & couching*

A ring of beads is threaded and secured round a single bead to form a flower head. The method is useful for beginners, as in the *Starter project,* also where many flowers need to be beaded, like the *Pinwheel for Christmas*. But you can also use the method for flowers in the Victorian style projects and the *Pin basket*.

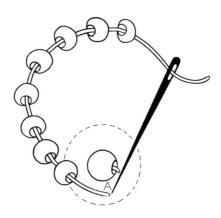

1. Threading the ring of beads
Double-stitch the centre bead. Bring up the needle at A inside the pattern marking, shown here by a broken circle. The distance between A and the centre bead should be half a bead width.

Thread enough beads to complete a circle within the pattern marking and insert the needle close to A. To finalise the number required, push the beads down to the base of the thread, and lay them just inside the pattern marking. You can adjust the number of beads at this stage if necessary. Take the needle through and gently pull the thread taut.

◀

Pl 8. Periwinkle – practice piece for *straight-stitching* triangular petals
Worked with larger beads on lined silk, but unlined calico or denim are equally suitable. Beads are size 9° and widely available in Güttermann tubes.

Trace and transfer the embroidery outline, p.67. See also *Stitches for starting and fastening off threads*. **Double-stitch** the centre bead. **Single-stitch** the first row of five single beads, spacing them evenly round the centre. **Straight-stitch** a second row of two beads to fit snugly against the first row. Finally work the third, outer row similarly, with three beads per petal. Use this photograph, and Fig 3 in the *Periwinkle* project as a guide.

Use this exercise to practise the flowers for the *Greetings card* and *Small pouch with flower* projects, but work only two rows of beads.

Normally the centre bead is slightly larger than the rest, see *Periwinkle* project. When using same size beads, as here, leave a small gap between the centre bead and the first row of beads around it for a more natural look.

The skill lies in spacing the petals evenly, which requires practice and a little patience!

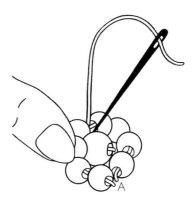

2. Securing the ring of beads
Hold the ring temporarily with your thumb so the beads fit snugly round the centre bead.

Bring up the needle outside the ring between two beads at a point opposite A. To secure the circle work a *couching stitch* over the core thread. Make two further couching stitches round the ring, each between a pair of beads.

Standard method – ***back-stitching***

A single bead is used for the centre, surrounded by a ring of ***back-stitched*** beads for the petals. Thus the petal beads are slightly separated from each other to give a natural look, Fig 3.

The Victorian style designs and the *Pin basket* were worked by this method.

Note. Tiny old seed beads, to be found at antiques fairs and charity shops, can add an authentic look to your embroidery. A yellow or gold seed bead as flower centre surrounded by mat white petals can also give a natural look.

Double-stitch the centre bead, Fig 1, then back-stitch the ring of petals, Fig 2.

Points to remember. The number of beads needed to fill the ring of petals will depend on their size. Here seven seed beads, size 15°, were used, but bead size can vary slightly even within a given range, so chose with care. If in doubt use fewer beads rather than more. To practise your flowers see Pl 9 opposite.

1. Double-stitching the centre bead

The single dot shows the centre, the broken circle shows the position of the ring of petals.

Double-stitch the central bead horizontally from *A-B* as shown.

2. Back-stitching the ring of beads

a. Securing the first petal bead with a *single stitch*

The centre bead is in position. Bring up the needle at any point on the circle, here at *C*. Thread a bead and take down the needle at *D*. Make sure the length of the stitch, *C-D*, matches the length of the bead hole.

b. *Back stitching* the remaining petal beads

Stitch the second and remaining beads anti-clockwise towards the first bead, shown by the arrow.

Bring up the needle at *E* and thread on a bead, matching the length of the stitch *E-D* to the length of the bead hole. Take down the needle close to *D*, allowing a slight gap to avoid piercing the thread of the previous stitch there, as this will weaken it. Continue back-stitching the beads all the way round, using the circle as a guide.

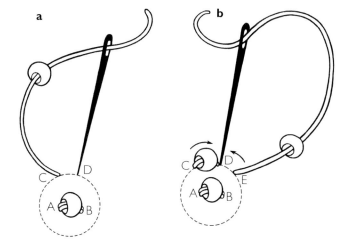

3. Completed flower head

Note the slight spacing between beads.

Pl 9. Ring of flowers with six petals – practice piece with the *Standard method*

Worked with larger beads on unlined soft denim. Beads are size 11° and widely available.

Dots represent the centres of flowers, circles represent the rings of six petals.

Trace and transfer the embroidery outline, p.67. See also *Stitches for starting and fastening off threads*. Use the finished embroidery as a guide and follow Figs 1-3 opposite.

Back-stitching the beads for the ring of petals will achieve a more realistic look than the quick method.

Applies also to the Lotus flower centre.

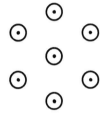

Embroidery outline

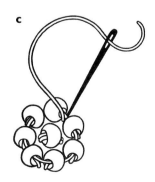

Tidying back-stitched beads by threading and couching

When a curve or ring of beads looks uneven, you can tidy it up by passing a thread through the beads and couching it down between them.

1. Tidying a ring of back-stitched beads

a. A ring of beads before tidying
Bring up the needle at *C* and start threading the ring as you would a necklace.

b. Completed threading
After threading the beads take the needle down close to *C* and pull the thread taut through the beads. This will slightly tighten the ring.

c. Couching between the threaded beads
Bring up the thread inside the ring and work a couching stitch across the thread between each pair of beads.

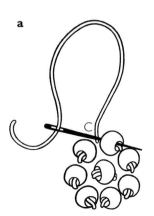

Beaded lotus flower

The following beading stitches are used in the *Beaded lotus* projects and the *Green pin wheel for Christmas*, which are intended for experienced embroiderers. They are explained in *Stitches used for lotus projects*.

- Stitching bugle beads on petals and leaves, p.47
- Edging petals and leaves with purl, p.47
- Adding a single bead to a leaf tip, p.48
- Making a small stitch with purl, p.49

Embroidery stitches

For couching, the needle needs to pass *vertically up and down* through a stretched fabric, which can only be achieved on a hoop. When couching metallic thread the fabric must be taut, but not as tight as for stitching beads.

Try practising couching by working the *Practice piece* below.

COUCHING METALLIC THREADS – CORD OR FLOSS

Stems in most projects are embroidered by couching a metallic thread (the *laid thread*) with viscose thread (the *couching thread*). The laid thread and the couching thread are each worked with their own needle.

The metallic thread is brought up from the back of the fabric, lightly held in place with the thumb and couched along the stem line.

The couching thread is worked from the back of the fabric. It is taken up and over the metallic thread and down again, to form couching stitches.

Stems are worked before other parts of the pattern, unless a flower lies across the stem. For Victorian projects start at the top of the longest stem and work the shorter or diagonal ones. For the Lotus projects it is easier to start at the flatter end of a stem and finish at the coiled end.

Allow an extra 5 cm (2 in) of metallic thread, and for couching use a 25 cm (10 in) long viscose thread with a knot at one end.

Work towards you, whenever possible.

In Figs 2-5 the metallic thread being couched is marked with diagonal lines, and a broken line shows the stem line. Figs 4 and 6 show the back of the fabric where the couching stitches are slanted.

Couching along straight or gently curved stems

Most straight or slightly curved stems are found in the Victorian style projects, but the method also applies to couching in other projects. A practice piece to couch a stem of *coton perlé* is given in Pl 10.

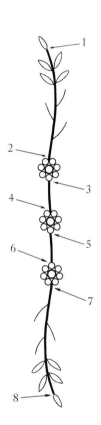

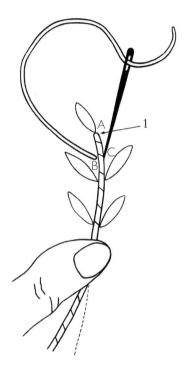

2. Couching a strand of metallic thread along a straight or slightly curved stem (enlarged)

The stem is shown by the broken line. The pointed ovals indicate buds.

Bring up the needle with the metallic thread at A, leaving a tail end of about 2 cm (¾ in) at the back of the fabric. Lay the metallic thread along the stem line holding it lightly with your thumb.

Bring up the couching thread about 3 mm (⅛ in) away from A, at B. Insert the needle *vertically* at C so the couching stitch will lie at right angles to the metallic thread.

Make sure the distance B-C matches the thickness of the metallic thread, and gently pull down the thread to form the first couching stitch.

Space further couching stitches at about 3 mm (⅛ in) intervals, Fig 3, making sure they lie at right angles to the metallic thread.

1. Stages of couching a stem

This simulates the main stem of the Victorian style *Needle book*, where the three flowers lying across the stem are worked first.

Use a continuous length of metallic thread for the whole stem. Points *1–8* show the order of working and where the metallic thread is plunged through the fabric.

Starting at the top, bring up the metallic thread at *1*, plunge it to the back at *2*, bring it up again at *3*, and so on down the stem.

To complete the rest of the stem follow the beading diagram for your project.

Plunging the couched thread to the back of the fabric

When the couching reaches a worked flower the metallic thread must be plunged just before the flower, and brought up again just after.

Note. At the back of the fabric you can pass both threads up to 6 mm (¼ in) between parts of the design without fastening off; this reduces the need for tidying thread ends.

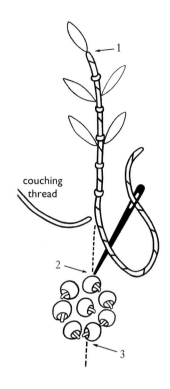

couching thread

3. Plunging a metallic thread ▶

Couch the thread up to a worked flower, here point *2*. Lay the couching thread temporarily to one side. Plunge the thread to the back of the fabric close to the beaded flower, as shown, and bring it up beyond it, at *3*.

Near point *2* work a final couching stitch and take the couching thread to the back of the fabric.

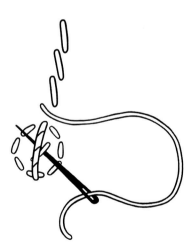

4. Making a whip stitch on the *back* of the fabric over a stitched area

Shows the back of the fabric with a ring of beading stitches and three couching stitches above.

Pass the couching thread under the central beading stitch and metallic thread to form a loop. This will bind the two threads together. Bring up the couching thread along the stem line, at *D*, Fig 5.

5. Continuing the couching

The metallic thread is shown at *3*, ready for couching. Bring up the couching thread along the stem line, about 3 mm (⅛ in) away from point *3*, as shown. Continue couching the metallic thread, plunging it behind further beaded flowers, to the end of the stem, *8* in Fig 1.

Pl 10. Couching threads – practice piece with *coton perlé* thread

The method of couching is the same for fibre and metallic threads, but it will be easier to practise with a thicker cotton thread couched on fine denim or calico, rather than on fine silk. Use of contrasting colours helps with spacing.

Yellow *coton perlé* thread, size 8, was couched with a single strand of red embroidery cotton. The flowers and buds were beaded with gold and mat red seed beads, size 8°, on fine indigo denim (unlined).

Dots represent the centres of the flowers, circles represent the rings of six petals, and the pointed ovals are buds.

Trace and transfer the embroidery outline, p.67. See also *Stitches for starting and fastening off threads*. Use the photograph as a guide. Couch the stems, as directed in this section, and Figs 2, 3 and 6. Bead the flowers using the *Quicker method*. Bead the buds along the stems by **threading and couching**. See also *Points to remember* below.

Embroidery outline

Tidying the ends of couched thread with whip stitches and a knotting stitch

This is done at the back of the fabric to secure the ends and avoid a tangle. The ends of the metallic thread are anchored to the stitching with several whip stitches worked with the couching thread, which is then tied with a **knotting stitch** and cut off, Fig 6. This applies to both straight and curved outlines.

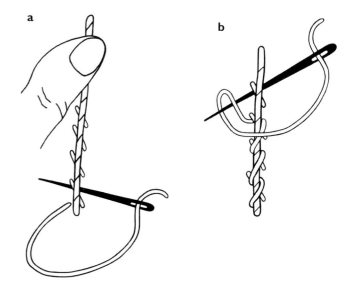

6. Tidying ends of couched threads

a. Starting a whip stitch over an end of metallic thread
Shows the back of the fabric and the end of a stem, e.g. point 8, Fig 1. While the end of the metallic thread is held in place over a row of couching stitches, the couching thread begins the first whip stitch.

   Pass the couching thread under the last stitch and the metallic thread. Pull the thread through to bind the two in a whip stitch.

b. Further whip stitches and a knotting stitch
Work several whip stitches, taking care not to pierce the silk. Make a loop behind the tip of the needle, as shown, and pull the thread through to create a knot. Trim off the tails of both threads.

Couching along curved stems

Some stems are more curved, especially those of the Beaded lotus projects, and require closer couching stitches. Their spacing will range from about 3 mm (⅛ in) along a straight line to about 1 mm on the tightest scrolls, with about 2 mm around the curve in Fig 7. Make sure that each couching stitch is at a right angle to the metallic thread.

Couching round tight scrolls

This technique applies to the scrolled tips of stems and tendrils. It is explained in *Stitches in lotus projects*, p.48.

7. Couching a metallic thread around a curve
Make the stitches slightly closer as the curve tightens.
To create a smoothly curved line keep a fairly firm tension on the couching thread but a looser tension on the metallic thread.

Points to remember for couching

- *Fabric.* Keep the fabric in the hoop taut but not drum tight. Over-tensioning the fabric will cause the couched metallic thread to pucker when the hoop is removed. The fabric can stretch, but the metallic thread does not.
- *Couching thread.* A 25 cm (10 in) long viscose thread is sufficient for the projects in this book, and should not be exceeded.
- The couching stitches should match the width of the metallic thread. Too narrow a stitch stops the metallic thread from lying flat on the silk. Too wide a stitch makes the stem look untidy. Gauging the width of couching stitches comes after a little practice!
- The couching stitches should hold the metallic thread closely but not too tightly. Over-tight stitches can dent the metallic thread. To tighten a slack couching thread after a stitch, work a back-stitch along the stem line on the back of the fabric.
- Practising the even spacing of couching stitches is easier with a couching thread of contrasting colour, as in Pl 10, p.87.

EMBROIDERING WITH COTTON OR SILK THREADS
Stem stitch
This stitch is widely used for plant stems! It is used for the stem of the *Periwinkle* project, and the central veins of the *Pin basket*, where it is explained.

Satin stitch
Satin stitch is worked in very close parallel stitches. It is used for the leaves of the *Pin basket*, where it is explained.

Edgings and sewing stitches

EDGING WITH BEADS
Picot edging

Picot edging can be seen on various 19th century accessories and was used on the original version of the Victorian style needle book. Picot edging is used on both needle book projects and on the key fob and one bodkin holder. As an edging to collars and cuffs it can make a distinctive fashion statement.

You will need
The completed embroidery mounted on board; short beading needle size 12; Nymo thread matching the silk fabric; seed beads 15°, in two colours selected from the project; ruler or tape measure.

Working notes
The edging is worked from the *back* of the panel, Figs 1-5. For a *needle book*, the edging is worked first along the bottom short edge, the long outer edge and the top edge of the Front panel: the spine edging is worked only after the spine has been stitched to the Front panel.

Picot edging for Needle book
Start with the Front panel. Flip it vertically, so you are looking at the back. What was previously the bottom short edge is now at the top. Work three edges clockwise from the top left, see Figs 1-5. The fourth (spine) edge will be worked after the Front is joined to the spine. Beads of a contrasting colour are shown shaded.

Spacing between picots is 3.5 mm (just over ⅛ in). Consistent spacing is important for a good appearance, though 0.5 mm adjustment is possible to position the corner beads correctly, Fig 5. A card strip marked in 3.5 mm divisions will help you plan, and picot positions can be marked with a dot.

On each diagram note the angle of the needle, taking care to slide it between the fabric and the board.

Pl 11. Completed needle book with picot edging
Worked from the back, the bottom edge was beaded first, then the front and top edges. The spine picots were worked after the Front panel was joined to the spine strip.

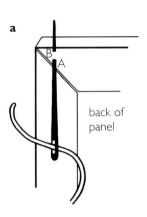

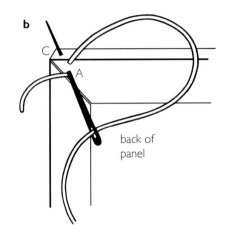

back of
panel

back of
panel

1. Starting with a simple back-stitch
(A knotted back-stitch is too bulky)

a. Pass the needle from *A* to *B*, sliding it under the fabric. Try to avoid stitching through the board.

b. Insert the needle back at *A* and bring it up near the corner of the top edge, at *C*. Pull on the thread gently to tension the **back-stitch** and secure the thread.

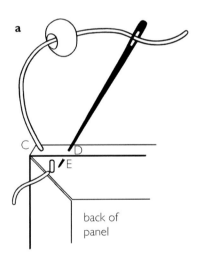

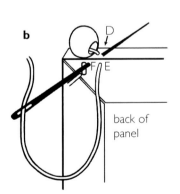

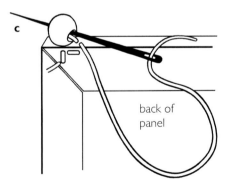

back of
panel

back of
panel

back of
panel

2. Securing the first bead

a. Bring the thread up inside the corner, at *C*. Thread on a bead. Insert the needle at *D* and bring it up below the upper edge at *E*.

b. Trim the end of the starter thread at *A* to prevent tangling. Gently tension the thread to sit the bead snugly on the edge. Insert the needle, sliding it under the fabric at *F* and up again at *D*.

c. Thread the needle back through the bead and slide the bead into a flat position, as shown in Fig 3.

Selecting beads for picots

To keep the picot symmetrical make sure the second and fourth beads match in size. Thread beads 2, 3 and 4 on to the needle to check. Bead sizes can vary, even in the same packet! If necessary adjust the order.

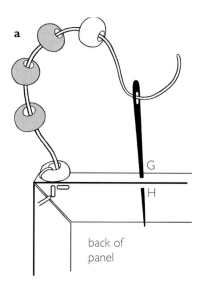

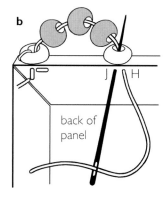

3. Making the first picot

a. Thread on 3 beads of a different colour, and a single bead matching the bead already secured. Insert the needle under the fabric at G and bring it through at H. The length of the first picot should be 3.5 mm (just over (⅛ in).

b. Insert the needle close to H at J, and bring it up through the last bead. Pull the thread taut through the beads. The beads should sit firmly and form a triangle with the base, see Fig 4

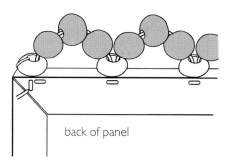

4. Making the next picots

Repeat the procedure of Fig 3.

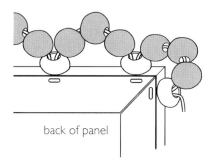

back of panel

Pl 12. Beaded picot edging worked by Lynette Williams (enlarged)

5. Working a picot round a corner

When planning the bead spacing, make sure the final bead of the last picot is positioned close to the corner. For the corner picot the first and last beads are stitched closer together, on either side of the corner.

Picot edging for Key fob or scissors keep

Complete the accessory including the twisted cord loop, and tassel if required. Work the picots clockwise round the edges following the method described above for needle books, Figs 1-5. Pl 5, p.59 and Pl 12 show finished corners.

For a *Key fob or scissors keep*, the edging is started at the corner, just after the point where the loop of twisted cord is attached. It is continued clockwise all round the edges and finished on the starting corner just before the twisted cord.

Flat beaded edging

This is used for the *Flower card*, *Pin cushion* and *Small pouch*. Stitches securing the edging are worked from the back of the panel (*Flower card*) or along the oversewn edges (*Pin cushion* and *Small pouch*). It makes an effective edging for miniature and fashion items.

back of panel or of oversewn edges

1. Flat beaded edging

The unshaded beads anchor the edging. Work in the direction of the arrows. Start at A with a **back-stitch**, Fig 1 above. Select two colours from your project. Thread on three beads of one colour and one of the other colour. Take the needle down at B to make a stitch at C. Take the needle up at D, through the bead once more, and thread on four more beads to repeat the process. Continue clockwise round the edges.

Triple-bead edging

Sets of three beads are *Straight-stitched* with a small gap (about the width of a bead) between sets. This edging decorates the edges of the *Pin basket*.

Beaded blanket stitch

This version of standard blanket stitch combines thread and beads to make an effective edging. It is used for the *Tassel*, Fig 6, p.62.

EDGING WITH THREADS
Twisted cord

A twisted cord is simple in construction yet effective in use. It makes an attractive edging, ties for a needle book or bodkin case, or loops for a key fob or tassel.

For these accessories use 3 to 5 strands of embroidery silk. To make a cord for the small purse in the *Starter project* use 3 strands of *coton perlé*, size 5. The more strands, the thicker the cord. The thread required will be about 3 times the length of the cord.

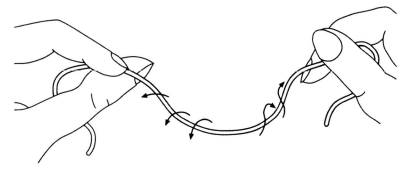

1. Starting to twist the thread
Take each end between thumb and index finger and twist the thread in opposite directions, as shown by the arrows. You can work alone or ask a friend to twist from one end.

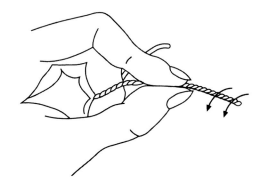

2. Tightening the twist
To obtain as tight a twist as possible trap the end of the twisted thread between the middle and fourth fingers. This will secure the twist so you can move your thumb and index finger to a new position.

As you continue twisting, tension the thread between your hands, otherwise it will start to twist on itself.

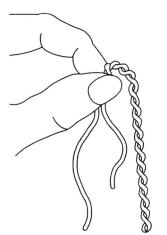

3. Completing the cord
Get a friend to hold the middle temporarily while you bring the two ends together, holding them firmly between thumb and index finger.

Once the middle is released, a twisted cord will form automatically. You will find the cord is tighter at the closed end. Continue to hold the open end, and even out the cord by running it between the thumb and index finger of your free hand. Tie a knot at the open end to prevent the cord unravelling.

Twisting 2.5 m of coton perlé for the Starter project
Work with a friend. Fold the length in half and simultaneously twist each end clockwise until it feels quite taut. Proceed as for the silk cord.

Sewing stitches

Oversewing
This joins two edges with a row of tiny stitches. It is worked on the right side of the fabric and used mainly in making up, e.g. joining the Front, Spine and Back in the *Needle books*. Before stitching, secure the edges close together with fine pins. Use a fine needle, and viscose or silk thread matching the fabric.

Blanket stitch
Standard blanket stitch was used in making up the *Pin wheel* and the *Pin basket*.

Stab stitch
This stitch is used to pass a thread through several layers of fabric and is used in the *Tassel*.

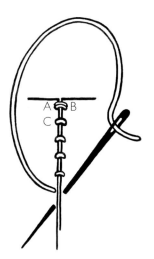

1. Working a row of oversewing
Secure the thread with two stitches at the top, *A-B*. Bring up the needle at *C* and continue working down the edge with even stitches, at right angles to the edge. Take care that only the horizontal part of the stitch is visible.

Needle books – making up

These instructions apply to both needle books, though the Lotus version is larger. Each has a Front and Back panel, spine, lining paper, fine woollen needle pages, and ribbon or twisted cord ties.

The stages of making up are:
- cutting and padding boards for the Front and Back
- mounting the embroidery on the padded Front, and the silk on the Back
- edging three sides of the Front panel
- cutting out and lining the spine
- attaching the spine to the Front panel
- edging the spine
- attaching the spine to the Back panel
- attaching the lining, needle pages and ties.

You will need

Tools and materials. Metal ruler, craft knife with sharp blade, cutting surface or board, sharp HB pencil; mounting board (as for picture framing), adhesive (e.g. PVA glue), cotton buds, tweezers, paper towels for cleaning up; embroidery scissors, fine pins (silk pins)*, short beading needle size 12, fine sewing needle.

Fabric. Calico or firm cotton strip to line the spine; polyester felt to pad the Front and Back, plain weave fine woollen fabric and cotton thread for needle pages, narrow ribbon 30 cm (12 in) long for ties.

Beads. For the picot edging: seed beads, 15°, in two of the colours used for the embroidery.

Threads. Nymo beading thread, viscose or silk sewing thread.

Lining. Lining paper matching the silk fabric or the beads, glue stick.

* dressmaker's pins are too thick!

Working notes

FRONT AND BACK PANELS

Padding the boards with felt. Always work on a clean surface.

1. Measure the solid outline of the Front or Back on your layout diagram, p.72. Use the measurements to mark two outlines on the mounting board and cut them out on a cutting board with a craft knife and metal ruler. Make sure the corners are right angles and the pieces of board match.

2. Use a cotton bud to apply a thin layer of adhesive to one surface. Place the board on the felt, adhesive side down, and let it set. Trim the felt to the board.

3. Repeat for the Back board and set aside. Don't cut out any pattern parts yet!

Mounting the embroidery on the padded Front

4. Centre the embroidery over the padded board and pin it in the order shown in Fig 1. The method of pinning, from one side to the point directly opposite (on the straight grain), is important for an even finish. Turn over the Front and cut round the tacked outline.

5. Following Figs 2 and 3, glue the edges and corners. Remove the pins.

Mounting the plain silk on to the padded Back

6. Follow the method of Figs 1-3.

Edging three sides of the Front panel

7. Work a ***picot edging*** on three sides of the Front, or if you prefer apply a ***flat beaded edging*** or ***twisted cord***.

SPINE

This will comprise a strip of silk, already lined, and a thin strip of calico. Follow Fig 4.

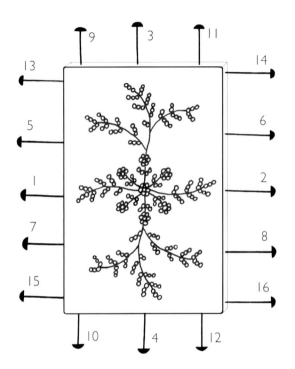

1. Pinning the Front

Centre the embroidery over the padded board, and check by holding both up to the light.

Insert a pin into the edge of the mounting board at *1*. At *2* opposite, gently pull the silk taut against pin *1* and insert pin *2*. Pin the short edges at *3* and *4* in the same way. Continue pinning towards the corners, working in the order shown. Check the centering as you go and adjust the pins if necessary.

Turn over the Front and trim the surrounding silk along the tacked outline, which allows 6 mm (¼ in) overlap, but avoid dislodging the pins.

2. Gluing the edges to the back of the board

This shows the back of the work. Apply a thin layer of adhesive from *A* to *B*, avoiding the corners. Behind pin *2* draw the silk down on to the adhesive with tweezers, pulling it taut against the board edge. Working out from the middle, press down and smooth out the silk with the flat side of the tweezers, keeping it taut against the board edge. Repeat the process for the opposite edge, then for the shorter edges. Remove the pins.

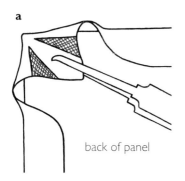

a

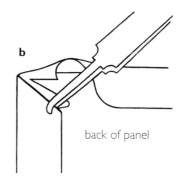

b

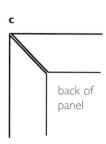

c

back of panel

back of panel

back of panel

3. Gluing the corners

a. Apply a small dab of adhesive to the board with a cotton bud near one corner.

Pull the silk taut diagonally across the corner and press down. Fold under the spare silk to form a temporary mitred edge and crease it. This will define triangles which you can snip away to reduce bulk, shown cross-hatched.

b. Apply a further dab of glue at the corner. Stick down the loose silk from the left side as shown, turning it under to lie at 45° to the edges. Repeat for the right hand side.

c. The mitred edge. Repeat the process for the other corners.

Making up the spine

8. Cut the silk along the tacked outline of the spine.

9. Cut a 5 mm (³/₁₆ in) wide strip of calico to slightly under the length of the mounted panels. The adhesive will cause the calico to stretch a little!

10. Make up the spine as shown in Fig 4b.

Attaching the spine to the Front panel, completing the picot edging

11. With wrong sides together, **oversew** the creased long edge of the spine to the Front in small neat stitches, and work a picot edging along it. This completes the edging of the Front.

12. Fold the other long edge over the calico, making a sharp crease. Join the creased edge to the Back by oversewing. The finished spine should be about 5 mm (³/₁₆ in) wide.

Adding ribbon ties (optional)

13. Cut two 115 mm (4½ in) lengths of ribbon, about 3 mm (⅛ in) wide. Lay the needle book face down on a clean surface. Before lining it secure the ties on the inside, Fig 5.

Lining the interior, making needle pages

14. *Paper lining.* Measure the internal dimensions of the needle book and prepare the lining, Pl 13.

a

b

4. Making the spine

a. Gluing the calico lining

Spine with glued calico lining. The clear area is the calico and the shaded area the lined back of the silk.

Apply a thin layer of adhesive evenly to one surface of the calico with a cotton bud.

Centre the calico, adhesive side down, on the lined back of the silk as shown. Press it lightly into position and let it set.

b. Folding and gluing the short ends of the spine

The darker shaded areas show the short ends of the spine glued over the calico.

With the calico strip facing you, apply a thin layer of adhesive to one short end of the silk. Fold the silk over the edge of the calico. Repeat for the other end and check the final length matches the panels. The folds provide a firm edge for the top and bottom of the spine, now ready to be attached to the Front. Fold one long edge over the calico, leaving a sharply creased edge.

15. *Needle pages*, see Pl 13.

16. Close the needle book, tie the ribbon ends in a bow and trim if necessary. Trimming the ends of the ribbon diagonally will reduce fraying. You can use **twisted cord** as ties if you prefer.

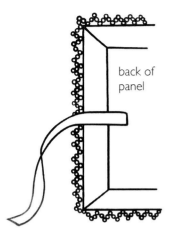

back of
panel

5. Securing the ribbon ties – shown from inside the Front
Mark the centre edge of the board inside the Front. Apply glue to one end of the ribbon for about 15 mm (½ in) and press down into position as shown. Repeat for the Back panel with the other tie.

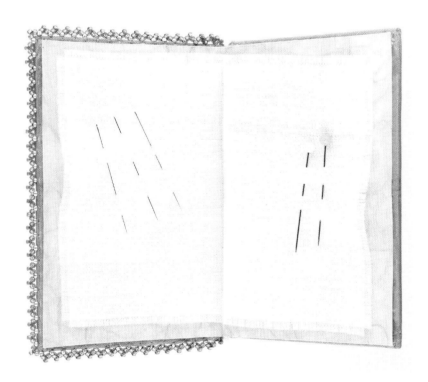

Pl 13. Inside the needle book – paper lining and needle pages

Mark a rectangle on the lining paper slightly smaller than the finished Front, Back and spine combined. Cut the lining paper, ensuring the edges are straight and the corners at right angles. Fold down the middle. For silk paper, as illustrated, line first with plain white paper.

Cut a piece of fine plain weave wool, or calico, slightly smaller than the lining paper. Remove four or five threads from each edge to leave a fringe. Fold down the middle of the wool to match the fold of the paper lining. Stitch the needle pages to the lining paper, along the fold, with small running stitches. Glue the lining paper to Front and Back with a glue stick.

Scissors case – making up

The case has five components: Front, Back, lining for each, and a twisted cord for edging.

The stages of making up include:
- padding the boards for Front and Back
- mounting the embroidery on the Front
- mounting the silk on the inner Back
- securing the lining to Front and Back
- securing the twisted cord to Front top edge
- joining the Front and Back
- finishing the edging

You will need:

Tools and materials. Sharp HB pencil, tracing paper; Dutch grey board* (445 gsm), scissors for cutting the board, adhesive (e.g. PVA glue), cotton buds, tweezers, paper towels for cleaning up; embroidery scissors, fine pins (silk pins)**, fine sewing needle.
Fabric. Small piece of extra heavy sew-in vilene or pellon to pad the Front and Back.
Threads. Viscose or silk sewing thread, embroidery silk for twisted cord.

* found as backing on memo pads. ** dressmaker's pins are too thick!

Working notes

Front and Back panels

Padding the boards. The outer Front and inner Back will be padded. Always work on a clean surface.

1. Carefully trace on to tracing paper the solid outline of the Front from the layout diagram, p.71. Turn over the tracing and place it, pencil side down, on the board. Transfer the outline to the board by tracing over it.
2. Cut out the board shape roughly, just outside the pencil outline. Now cut out the shape accurately, using the middle of the blade.
3. Repeat for the Back. The common sections of Front and Back should match closely.

4. *Outer Front.* With the longer edge on the left apply a thin layer of adhesive over the surface with a cotton bud. Place the board on the padding, adhesive side down, and let it set. Trim the padding to the board.
5. *Inner Back.* Repeat for the Back and set aside. *Don't* cut out any pattern parts yet.

Mounting the embroidery on the outer Front
6. Centre the embroidery over the padded board and pin it in the order shown in Fig 1. The method of pinning, from one side to the point directly opposite (on the straight grain), is important for an even finish.
7. Turn over the panel. Trim the surrounding fabric by cutting along the tacked outline on your silk, which allows 6 mm (¼ in) overlap. Avoid dislodging the pins.
8. Cut notches into the edges of the overlap and glue down, see Fig 2. Remove the pins.

Mounting the silk on the inner Back
9. Follow directions 6-8 above with Figs 3 and 4 instead of Fig 2.

Securing the lining to the Front and Back
10. *Front.* Cut out the inner Front, using the tacked outline on your silk as a guide. This allows 6 mm (¼ in) overlap. Cut notches round the edges of the silk, *slightly shorter* than those on the embroidered Front, Fig 2.
11. Fold the overlap under and align the fold with the edge on the back of the panel. Pin the folded edge, section by section, into the embroidery overlap in the order shown in Fig 2. Adjust the pins if necessary so the lining is stretched evenly. Push the pin heads right in and **oversew** the two edges. Remove the pins.
12. *Back.* Repeat for the Back using directions *10 & 11,* but with Fig 4 in place of Fig 2 as a guide.

continued on p.103

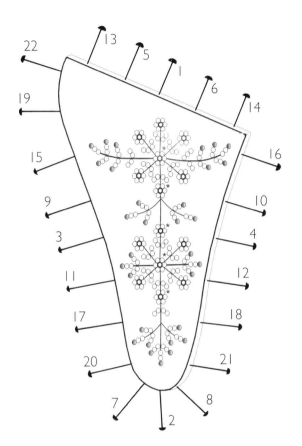

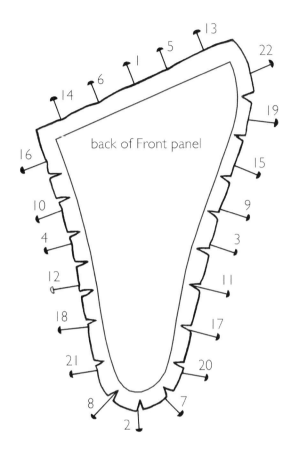

back of Front panel

1. Pinning the Front to the padded board

Centre the embroidery over the padded board, and check by holding both up to the light.

Insert a pin into the middle upper edge of the padded board at *1*. Opposite, on the base, gently pull the fabric taut against pin *1* and insert pin *2*. Next pin *3* and *4*, then continue pinning in the order shown. Check the centering as you go and adjust the pins if necessary.

2. Gluing down the overlap on the Front panel

With the back of the board facing you, trim the surrounding fabric along the tacked outline, which allows 6 mm (¼ in) overlap, but avoid dislodging the pins. Cut notches into the edges, cutting *towards* the board edge, as shown, but *not* right up to it.

Starting with the top edge, apply thin dabs of adhesive to the board with the cotton bud, a section at a time avoiding the corners, and glue down the overlap with the help of tweezers, see Fig 2, p.97. Press down and smooth out the fabric with the flat side of the tweezers, pulling it taut against the board edge. For the corners see *Needle book – making up*, Fig 3, p.98. Clean off any surplus glue with a paper towel. Remove the pins.

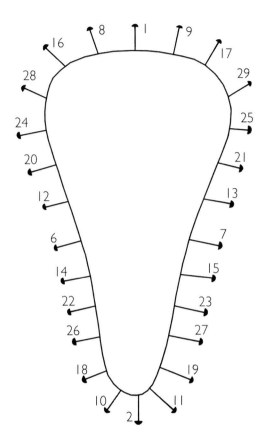

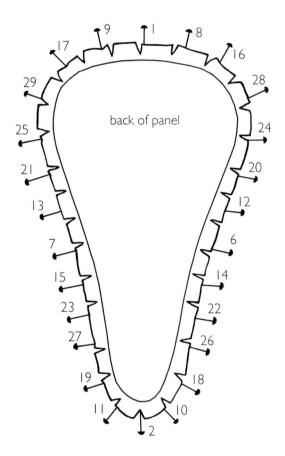

3. Pinning the silk to the inner Back padded board

Centre the silk over the padded board and pin the edges working in the order shown. Trim the silk leaving a 6 mm (¼ in) overlap.

4. Gluing the edges to the back of the board

With the back of the board facing you, cut notches into the edges, cutting *towards* the board edge as shown, but *not* right up to it. Starting with the top edge, apply thin dabs of adhesive to the board with the cotton bud, a section at a time, and glue down the overlap with the help of tweezers, as for Fig 2. Remove the pins.

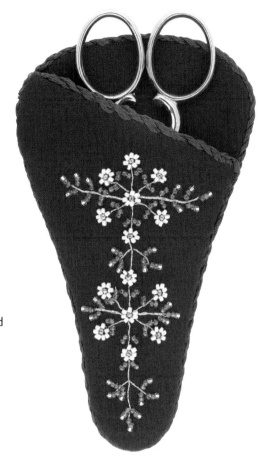

Pl 14. Completed scissors case edged with twisted cord
Start at the top left corner of the Front. Secure the cord along the diagonal edge, continue down and round the case, over the top and finish at the right end of the diagonal edge.

TWISTED CORD

13. Prepare a ***twisted cord*** with 4 strands of embroidery silk, long enough for the upper edge of the Front and all round the Back.

Edging and joining the Front and Back

14. Working from the top left corner and starting with the looped end of the twisted cord, couch with diagonal stitches along the upper edge of the Front. Use a matching viscose thread and lay the stitches in the grooves of the cord.

15. With inner sides together join the Front and Back panels by oversewing.

16. Couch the twisted cord all the way round the case. Bind the cord at the end of the length required and cut off the rest.

17. Tuck the bound end inside the lower end of the Front opening and secure it with a few stitches.

Bodkin & needle holder – making up

These instructions apply to both the Victorian style and Beaded lotus versions. The bellows-shaped bodkin holder has eight components: an outer (padded) and inner (unpadded) panel for the Front, and again for the Back; a hinge, needle page, edging and ties. See Pl 15.

The stages of making up are:
- tracing the outline and cutting the four boards
- padding the two outer boards (one Front, one Back)
- mounting the embroidery on the padded Front board
- mounting the silk on the padded Back board
- mounting the silk on the unpadded inner boards
- making the hinge and attaching it to the outer Front panel
- assembling and edging the Front
- making and securing the needle page
- attaching the hinge to the inner Back panel
- assembling and edging the Back
- preparing and securing the ties

You will need

Tools and materials. Sharp HB pencil, tracing paper; Dutch grey board* (445 gsm), scissors for cutting the board, adhesive (e.g. PVA glue), cotton buds, tweezers, paper towels for cleaning up; embroidery scissors, fine pins (silk pins)**, short beading needle size 12, fine sewing needle.
Fabric. Small piece of extra heavy sew-in vilene or pellon to pad the Front and Back, a small piece of fine felt for the needle page.
Threads. Nymo beading thread (Lotus version) and viscose or silk sewing thread (for both).
Edging. Embroidery silk (4 strands) for twisted cord (Victorian style version), or seed beads 15°, in two of the colours used for the embroidery (Lotus version).
Ties. Embroidery silk for twisted cord (Victorian), or narrow ribbon, 30 cm (12 in) long (Lotus).

* found as backing on memo pads. ** dressmaker's pins are too thick!

Working notes
FRONT AND BACK
Tracing the outline and cutting the four boards
Always work on a clean surface.
1. Carefully trace on to tracing paper the solid outline of the Front or Back on your layout diagram, p.70. Turn over the tracing and place it, pencil side down, on the board. Transfer the outline on to the board by retracing.
2. Cut out the shape roughly, just outside the pencil outline. Next cut out the shape closely following the pencil outline. Use the middle of the blade, not the tip of the scissors, for this. Repeat for the second board. Refine the shapes with further minimal trimming, making sure that the sides are symmetrical and the two boards are closely matched. Mark both *F*. These together will form the Front.
3. Carefully cut two more shapes, check they closely match the first two and mark both *B*. These together will form the Back.

Padding the outer boards for Front and Back
4. Use a cotton bud to apply a thin layer of adhesive to one surface of one Front board. Place the board on the padding, adhesive side down, and let it set. Trim the padding accurately to the board.
5. Repeat for one Back board. *Don't* cut out any patterns yet.

Mounting the embroidery on the (padded) Front board
6. Centre the embroidery over the padded board marked *F* and pin it in the order shown in Fig 1. The method of pinning, from one side to the point directly opposite (on the straight grain), is important for an even finish.
7. Turn over the work, trim the silk, cut notches into the overlap and glue it down. Follow Fig 2.

Mounting the silk on the (padded) Back board
8. Mount the plain silk on the padded board marked *B* following Figs 1 and 2, cutting notches as before. This will be the outer Back panel.

All diagrams shown reduced unless stated otherwise.

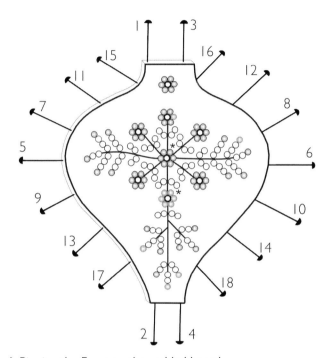

Mounting the silk on the (unpadded) inner boards
9. Cut out the tacked pattern outlines for the inner Front and inner Back panels. Lay one over the unpadded Front board *F*, and centre it. Pinning is unnecessary.
10. Cut notches, apply adhesive and glue down the overlap a section at a time, see Fig 2 (ignoring the pins shown).
11. Repeat for the unpadded Back board *B*. Your four panels are now complete.

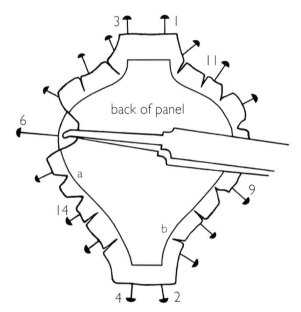

1. Pinning the Front to the padded board
Centre the embroidery over the padded board *F*, and check by holding both up to the light.

First insert a pin into the flat edge of the padded board at *1*. At *2* opposite, gently pull the fabric taut against pin *1* and insert pin *2*. Continue with *3* and *4*, then the widest points *5* and *6*, in the same way. Continue pinning in the order shown. Check the centering as you go and adjust the pins if necessary.

2. Gluing down the overlaps on the Front and Back outer panels
Work with the back facing you. Using the tacked outline on your silk as a guide, trim the surrounding fabric, which allows 6 mm (¼ in) overlap. Avoid dislodging the pins with the scissors.

Cut straight notches into the concave edges (like *b*), and V-shaped notches into the convex ones (like *a*). Cut *towards* the board edge, as shown, but *not* right up to it.

Apply thin dabs of adhesive to the board with the cotton bud, a section at a time avoiding the corners, and glue down the overlap with the help of tweezers. Starting from the widest point work along one edge and then the opposite edge. Press down and smooth out the fabric with the flat side of the tweezers, pulling it taut against the board edge. For the corners see *Needle book – making up*, Fig 3, p.98. Glue the top and bottom edges last. Clean off any surplus glue with a paper towel. Remove the pins.

Repeat the pinning (Fig 1) and gluing for the outer Back.

HINGE
Making and attaching to the outer Front panel
12. Make the hinge and glue it to the outer Front panel. Follow Figs 3 and 4. The other end will be glued later, see *17* below.

3. The hinge
a. Making the tube.
Cut out a 25×30 mm (1×1¼ in) rectangle from your interlined silk. Fold it in half lengthways with the right side together. Sew into a tube using running stitches leaving 4-5 mm (¼ in) overlaps.
b. The finished hinge.
Turn the tube right side out by attaching a small safety pin to one end and pushing it through. Spread the overlaps either side of the seam, and press the tube flat to form a thin rectangle with the seam lying centrally.

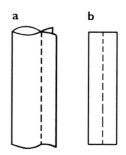

4. Gluing one end of the hinge
Lay the padded Front panel, embroidery side down, on a clean surface. Place just under half the length of the hinge, seam side up, on the base of the panel. Glue it to the board.

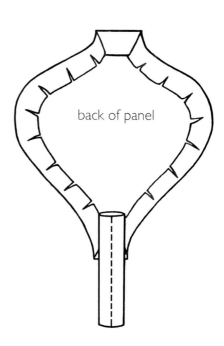

back of panel

Assembling and edging the Front
13. Join the two mounted panels (*F*) by **oversewing**, Fig 5. This will sandwich the end of the hinge already glued to the outer Front panel.
14. *Securing the twisted cord* (Victorian style project). Make a **twisted cord** with four strands of embroidery silk, long enough to go all the way round the panel. Use a matching viscose thread and couch the cord to the edge, Figs 5 and 6.
15. *Edging* (Lotus project). Edge the Front with **beaded picots**.

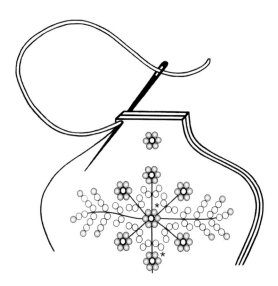

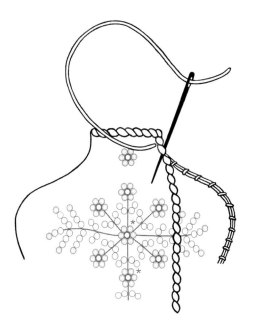

5. Assembling the Front

Place together the two mounted panels *(F)*, with wrong sides facing.

Secure your thread by making two stitches, one on top of the other, at the upper left corner on the embroidered side. *Oversew* the edges, stitching through both panels, including the hinge. Leave a small gap in the stitching just before the top left corner to accommodate the end of the twisted cord.

6. Attaching the twisted cord to the Front

Attach the looped end of the twisted cord at the upper left corner. Couch the cord round the edges, angling the thread between the twisted strands to hide the stitches. Ensure it passes in front of the hinge.

Just before completing the couching, bind the cord at the end of the length required and cut off the rest. Tuck the bound end into the gap left in the oversewing and complete the couching.

NEEDLE PAGE
Making and securing to the inner Back panel
16. Follow Fig 7, and see Pl 15.

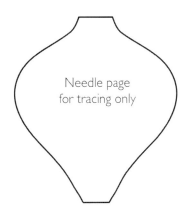

Needle page
for tracing only

7. Needle page – template ▶

Trace the template and pin it to the felt, then cut out the shape. Centre the needle page on the inner Back panel. Secure it at the top with a few stitches. Actual size.

17. Position the inner Back panel, wrong side up, against the assembled Front, leaving a 4 mm ($^3/_{16}$ in) section of the hinge free between them, see Fig 8. Glue the unattached end of the hinge to the Back panel.

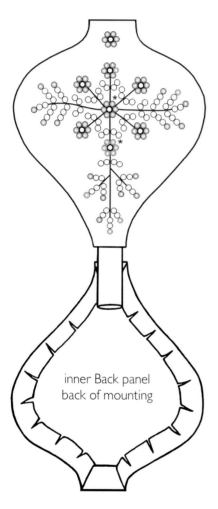

inner Back panel
back of mounting

18. Join the two panels for the Back, wrong sides together, by oversewing, Fig 9. The Back is edged only for the Victorian style project.

19. *Securing the twisted cord* (Victorian project). Repeat *14.* above. At the top and bottom edge secure the cord *only* to the outer panel, see Fig 9.

Needle page
secured to inner Back

8. Gluing the other end of the hinge

Lay the inner Back panel, needle page down, on a clean surface. Place the lower end of the Front, embroidery up, against the lower end of the inner Back panel. Leave a short length of hinge, about 4 mm ($^3/_{16}$ in), between the Front and Back as shown so they will close flat.

Glue the loose end of the hinge to the panel. Check that the gap is adequate by closing the bodkin holder before the glue sets. Seal the open end of the hinge with a dab of glue to prevent the bodkin penetrating the hinge.

9. Assembling and edging the Back

Follow Figs 5 and 6, as for the Front. At the top and bottom edges ensure you attach the cord to the padded panel *only*, leaving the opening free for the bodkin as shown.

Attach one twisted cord tie to the top edge of the inner Back panel, as shown, and the other to the Front top edge. Slide the bodkin through the gap between the two Back panels.

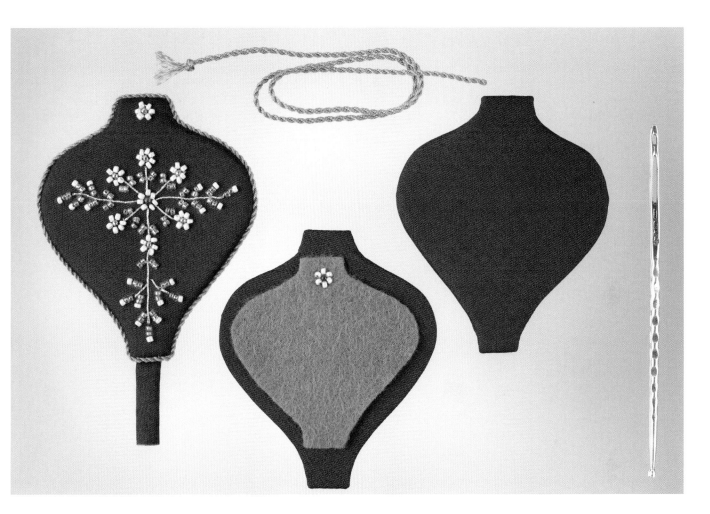

Pl 15. Partly assembled bodkin holder
Clockwise from left: Assembled Front panels with hinge (inner panel is hidden); twisted cord; padded outer Back; silver bodkin; inner Back panel with needle page.

You can embellish the needle page by working the beaded flower. This is worked in the hand rather than on a hoop.

TIES

20. *Twisted cord ties* (Victorian project). Make two lengths of twisted cord, each 15 cm (6 in) long. Attach one looped end to the Front top edge, and the other above the needle page on the inner Back panel, Fig 9.

21. *Ribbon ties* (Lotus project). Cut two 15 cm (6 in) lengths of ribbon about 7 mm (¼ in) wide. Fold the end under and secure each tie to the top edge. You can also embroider (in the hand) a ***beaded flower***, p.81, to the folded edge before securing the tie by oversewing.

Pin wheel – making up

These instructions apply to both the Lotus and Christmas pin wheels. The pin wheel components are: Front and Back panels, felt padding, covering and optional edging.

The stages of making up include:
- padding the boards for Front and Back
- mounting the embroidery on the Front
- mounting a second embroidery or plain silk on the Back
- preparing the layered felt padding
- securing the felt padding between Front and Back
- finishing the edge with ribbon
- edging with twisted cord (optional)

You will need

Tools and materials. Compasses, Dutch grey board* (445 gsm), scissors for cutting the board; adhesive (e.g. PVA glue), cotton buds, tweezers, paper towels for cleaning up; embroidery scissors, fine pins (silk pins)**, fine sewing needle.

Fabric. Small piece of extra heavy sew-in vilene or pellon to pad the Front and Back, a piece of felt for layered padding; 7 mm (¼ in) ribbon to match the fabric, 15 cm (6 in) long.

Threads. Viscose or silk sewing thread, and embroidery silk for the (optional) twisted cord, to match the fabric.

* found as backing on memo pads ** dressmaker's pins are too thick!

Working notes

Front and Back

Padding the boards. Always work on a clean surface.

1. Draw two circles of 19 mm (¾ in) radius on the board and cut them out carefully, using the middle of the blade rather than the tip of your scissors. The two discs must match.

2. Use one board as a template to cut out six matching felt discs for the padding. Set aside.

3. Apply a thin layer of adhesive with a cotton bud to one side of one board, right up to the edge. Place the board on the vilene interlining, adhesive side down, and let it set. Trim the interlining to the edge of the board.

4. Repeat for the second board.

Mounting the embroideries on the Front and Back

5. Centre the embroidery over the padded board and pin it in the order shown in Fig 1. The method of pinning, from one side to the point directly opposite (on the straight grain), is important for an even finish. Turn over the panel.

6. Trim the surrounding fabric, cut notches into the overlap and glue it to the back of the board, Fig 2.

7. Repeat stages 5 and 6 for the other embroidery, or for a plain silk Back.

Felt padding

Preparing the padding

8. Align the felt discs. As felt varies in thickness, and the layers will be compacted when they are stitched together, adjust the number of layers to the width of your ribbon, Fig 3.

9. Cover the edges of the padding with a strip of felt and **blanket-stitch** the edges, Fig 4.

Securing the padding between Front and Back

10. Lay the Front on a clean surface, embroidered side down, and apply a thin layer of adhesive with a cotton bud to the board centre. Centre the felt padding over the glued area and press into place: allow the glue to set. Repeat the procedure for the Back, to sandwich the padding between the panels.

continued on p.112

Diagrams not to scale

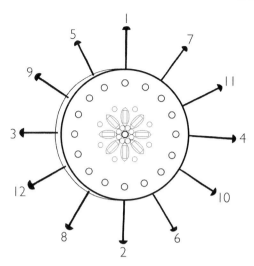

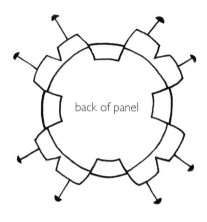

back of panel

1. Pinning the Front to the padded board

Centre the embroidery over the padded board, and check by holding both up to the light.

Insert a pin into the edge of the padded board at 1. At 2 opposite, gently pull the fabric taut against pin 1 and insert pin 2. Continue pinning in the same way in the order shown. Check the centering as you go and adjust the pins if necessary.

2. Gluing down the overlaps

Turn over the Front so the board side faces you. Trim the surrounding fabric along the tacked outline, which allows 6 mm (¼ in) overlap. Avoid dislodging the pins. Cut V-shaped notches *towards* the board edge, but *not* right up to it.

Apply thin dabs of adhesive to the board with the cotton bud, a small section at a time, and glue down the overlap with the help of tweezers. Press down and smooth out the fabric with the flat side of the tweezers, pulling it taut against the board edge. Clean off any surplus glue with a paper towel. Remove the pins.

Repeat the pinning (Fig 1) and gluing for the Back.

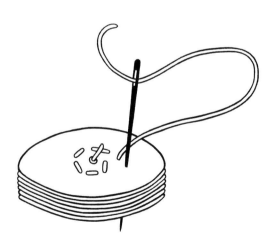

3. Preparing the felt padding

Six discs of felt are shown being stitched together. Starting in the centre with a knotted thread, work outwards in a spiral of running stitches through all layers to hold them together. Ensure the stitches are taut to compact the layers.

4. Covering the edges of the padding

Pin a strip of felt, slightly wider than the padding, round the circumference, pushing the pin heads right in. Trim any excess from the strip so that the ends butt together. Secure it round both edges with *blanket stitch*, as shown, and remove the pins.

EDGING

Covering the padding with ribbon

11. Pin the ribbon and **oversew** the edges, see Fig 5. Leave a small gap in the oversewing on each edge if you plan to edge with twisted cord. Remove the pins. Your pin wheel is ready to be filled with pins around the ribbon.

Optional twisted cord edging

12. The *Lotus pin wheel* has a **twisted cord** edging. Use two strands of silk for the cord, and couch it to the edges with diagonal stitches lying in the grooves of the cord. Bind the cord at the end of the required length and cut off the rest. Tuck the bound end inside the gap left when stitching the ribbon and secure with a few stitches.

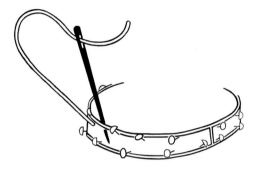

5. Covering the padding with ribbon
Pin the edges of the ribbon into the boards, alternating between top and bottom edges. Fold the ribbon ends under and secure the join with pins. Now push all the pin heads into the padding. **Oversew** both edges, but leave a slight gap to hide the bound end of a twisted cord if used. Oversew the join of the ribbon and remove the pins.

Pl 16. Completed pin wheel edged with twisted cord

Key fob or scissors keep – making up

The key fob is quite simple to construct. It can be used as a pendant or enlarged for a hanging. It comprises Front, Back, a twisted cord and an optional tassel. For a scissors keep, make the twisted cord longer.

The stages of making up include:
- padding the boards for the Front and Back
- mounting the embroidery on the Front
- mounting plain silk or a second embroidery on the Back
- joining the Front and Back panels
- securing the twisted cord loop
- working the picot edging
- securing the tassel.

You will need

Tools and materials. Dutch grey board* (445 gsm), ruler, sharp HB pencil, scissors for cutting the board, adhesive (e.g. PVA glue), cotton buds, tweezers, paper towels for cleaning up; embroidery scissors, fine pins (silk pins)**, fine sewing needle, short beading needle size 12.
Fabric. Small piece of extra heavy sew-in vilene or pellon to pad the Front and Back.
Beads. Seed beads, 15°, in two of the colours used for the embroidery.
Threads. Viscose or silk sewing thread; Nymo beading thread; embroidery silk for the twisted cord loop and tassel.

* found as backing on memo pads ** dressmaker's pins are too thick!

Working notes

FRONT AND BACK PANELS
Padding the boards. Always work on a clean surface.
1. Measure and cut two pieces of grey board, 2.6 cm (1 in) square. Make sure the pieces of board match and the corners are right angles.
2. Use a cotton bud to apply a thin layer of adhesive to one surface. Place the board on the padding, adhesive side down, and let it set. Trim the padding to the board.
3. Repeat for the other board and set aside.
Don't cut out either pattern part yet.

Mounting the embroidery on the Front
4. Centre the embroidery over the padded board and pin it in the order shown in Fig 1. The method of pinning, from one side to the point directly opposite (on the straight grain), is important for an even finish.
5. Turn over the panel, trim the silk, and glue down the overlap, following Fig 2. Remove the pins.

Mounting plain silk or a second embroidery on the Back
6. Follow the method of *4* and *5* above.

Joining and edging the Front and Back panels
7. Place the panels together with wrong sides facing and **oversew** the edges, leaving small gaps on two opposite corners.
8. Work a **picot edging** in the two bead colours, leaving gaps at the same corners, Pls 5 and 17.

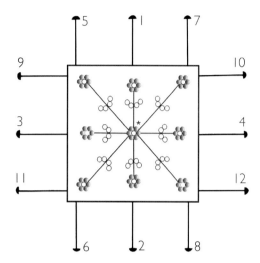

1. Pinning the Front and Back

Centre the embroidery over the padded board, and check by holding both up to the light.

Insert a pin into the edge of the board at *1*. At *2* opposite, gently pull the fabric taut against pin *1* and insert pin *2*. Pin the other edges at *3* and *4* in the same way. Continue pinning in the order shown. Check the centering as you go and adjust the pins if necessary.

Turn over the board and trim the surrounding fabric along the tacked outline, which allows 6 mm (¼ in) overlap. Avoid dislodging the pins.

2. Gluing the overlaps to the back of the board

This shows the back of the panel. Apply a thin layer of adhesive down the left side of the panel, *avoiding* the corners. Behind pin *4* draw the fabric down on to the adhesive with tweezers, pulling it taut against the board edge. Working out from the middle, press down and smooth out the fabric with the flat side of the tweezers. Repeat the process for the opposite edge, then the other edges. Remove the pins.

To glue the corners, see Fig 3 in *Needle books – making up*.

CORD AND TASSEL

9. Make a ***twisted cord*** with 4 strands of embroidery silk in a colour matching the fabric, about 3 cm (1¼ in) long for a key fob; or 18-20 cm (7-8 in) long for a scissors keep. Bind the cord at the end of the length required and cut off the rest. Tuck the ends of the cord between the two panels at a corner gap and secure with a few stitches.

10. Make a tassel if required, using the same embroidery silk as for the cord and secure it in the gap at the opposite corner.

Pl 17. The finished key fobs ▶

Note the gaps left at opposite corners in the picot edging to secure the tassel and cord. For a scissors keep or hanging make a longer cord.

Pin basket – making up

The pin basket components are: Front and Back panels, felt padding, ribbon edging and a handle.

The stages of making up include:
- padding the boards for Front and Back
- mounting embroidery on Front and Back
- preparing the layered felt padding
- securing the felt padding between Front and Back
- edging the basket with ribbon and beads
- making the handle

You will need

Tools and materials. Tracing paper, Dutch grey board* (445 gsm), dressmaker's carbon paper, sharp HB pencil, a strip of flexible card for the handle, scissors for cutting the board; adhesive (e.g. PVA glue), cotton buds, tweezers, paper towels for cleaning up; embroidery scissors, fine pins (silk pins)**, fine sewing needle, beading needles size 12.

Fabric. Small piece of extra heavy sew-in vilene or pellon to pad the Front and Back, a piece of felt for layered padding; 15 cm (6 in) of ribbon 7 mm (¼ in) wide to match the fabric.

Beads. Seed beads, 15°, in two of the colours used for the embroidery.

Threads. Viscose or silk sewing thread; Nymo beading thread.

* found as backing on memo pads ** dressmaker's pins are too thick!

Working notes

FRONT AND BACK

Tracing the outline and cutting the boards

Always work on a clean surface.

1. Carefully trace on to tracing paper the solid outline of the Front or Back on your layout diagram, p.69. Turn over the tracing and place it, pencil side down, on to the board. Transfer the outline on to the board by retracing.

2. Cut out the shape roughly, just outside the pencil outline. Next cut out the shape following the pencil outline closely. Use the middle of the blade, not the tip of the scissors, for this. Refine the shape with further minimal trimming, making sure that the sides are symmetrical.

3. Repeat for the second board; the two boards must match closely.

4. Use one board as a template to cut out six matching basket shapes from the felt for the padding. Set aside.

Padding the boards

5. Apply a thin layer of adhesive with a cotton bud to one side of one board, right up to the edge. Place the board on the vilene interlining, adhesive side down, and let it set. Trim the interlining to the edge of the board.

6. Repeat for the second board.

Mounting the embroideries

7. Centre the embroidery over the padded board and pin it in the order shown in Fig 1. The method of pinning, from one side to the point directly opposite (on the straight grain), is important for an even finish.

8. Trim the surrounding fabric, cut notches into the overlap and glue it to the back of the board, see Fig 2.

9. Repeat stages 7. and 8. for the other embroidery, or for a plain silk Back if you wish.

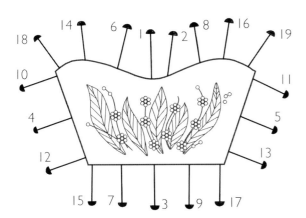

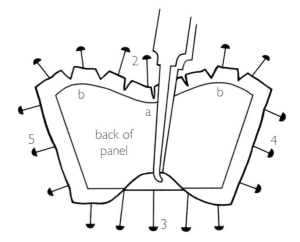

1. Pinning the Front to the padded board

Centre the embroidery over the padded board, and check by holding both up to the light.

Insert a pin into the edge of the padded board at *1* and *2*. At *3* opposite, gently pull the fabric taut against pin *1* and *2*, and insert pin *3*. Continue pinning in the same way in the order shown. Check the centering as you go and adjust the pins if necessary.

2. Gluing down the overlaps

Turn over the Front so the board side faces you. Trim the surrounding fabric along the tacked outline, which allows 6 mm (¼ in) overlap. Avoid dislodging the pins.

Cut straight notches into the concave edges (as at *a*), and V-shaped notches into the convex ones (as at *b*). Cut *towards* the board edge, as shown, but *not right up to it*.

Starting along the bottom edge but avoiding the corners, apply a smear of adhesive to the board with the cotton bud, and glue down the overlap with the help of tweezers. Press down and smooth out the fabric with the flat side of the tweezers, pulling it taut against the board edge.

Working out from the middle on the top edge, apply dabs of adhesive a section at a time and glue down the flaps. Glue the sides as for the bottom.

For the corners see *Needle book – making up*, Fig 3, p.98. Clean off any surplus glue with a paper towel. Remove the pins.

Repeat the pinning (Fig 1) and gluing for the Back.

FELT PADDING
Preparing the padding
10. Align the felt shapes. As felt varies in thickness, and the layers will be compacted when they are stitched together, adjust the number of layers to the width of your ribbon. Follow Fig 3a.

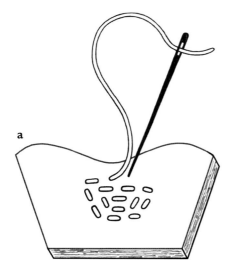

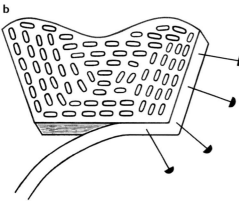

11. Cover the edges of the padding with a strip of felt, Fig 3b, and **blanket-stitch** the edges.

Securing the padding between Front and Back
12. Lay the Front panel on a clean surface, embroidered side down, and apply a thin layer of adhesive with a cotton bud to the board centre. Centre the felt padding over the glued area and press into place: allow the glue to set.
13. Repeat the procedure for the Back, to sandwich the padding.

EDGING
Edging the basket with ribbon
14. Pin the ribbon from *A* to *B*, Fig 4, and **oversew** its edges to the Front and Back with matching thread. Remove the pins. Pin and oversew another piece of ribbon along the top from *B* to *A*.

Oversew the joins at *A* and *B*. This provides a firm anchorage for the handle.

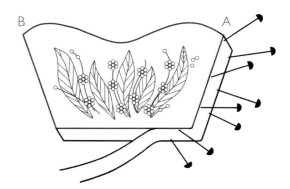

3. Felt padding
a. The layers are shown being stitched together. Starting in the centre with a knotted thread, work outwards in a spiral of running stitches through all layers to hold them together. Ensure the stitches cover the whole area to compact the padding.
b. Pin a strip of felt, slightly wider than the padding, round the basket shape, and push the pins right in once the strip is in place. Trim the strip so the ends butt together. Secure it along both edges with *blanket stitch*, see *Pin wheel – making up*, Fig 4, p.111, and remove the pins.

4. Edging the basket with ribbon
Turn the ribbon end under and, starting at *A*, pin the edges into the boards, alternating between Front and Back. Continue pinning around the flat edges of the basket to *B* and fold the other end under.

Push all the pin heads into the padding. *Oversew* along both edges. Pin another length of ribbon along the top edge of the basket, between *B* and *A*, turning under the ends and oversewing as before. Oversew the joins at *A* and *B*, where the handle will be secured. Remove the pins.

Triple bead edging

15. ***Straight-stitch*** sets of three beads round the edges of the basket, Fig 5.

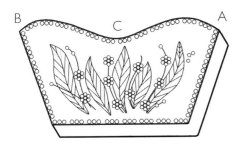

THE HANDLE

Preparing, beading and securing

16. Cut two 9 cm (3½ in) lengths of 7 mm (¼ in) wide ribbon, transfer the pattern to one of them and bead it, see Fig 6.

Turn the ends under on both ribbons, leaving an overall length of 8 cm (3⅛ in) for each. With the wrong sides together, ***oversew*** the long edges of the ribbons. Cut a strip of flexible card, 5-6 mm (¼ in) wide, to just under the handle length and slip it between the ribbons. Oversew the ends and secure the handle along the joins at *A* and *B*, Fig 5.

6. Beading the handle

a. Embroidery outline. Diagonal lines show the positions for *straight-stitched* beads. Tape one ribbon to a flat surface and transfer the embroidery outline with dressmaker's carbon paper. Actual size.

5. Finishing the Front with triple-bead edging
Straight-stitch sets of three beads centrally at *C* and work further sets along the top edges of the basket, first to *A* then left to *B*. The gaps should be about one bead width.

Work the bottom edge from the centre so its beading is also symmetrical. Work the sides from top to bottom. Bead the edges of the Back similarly. Note that the number of sets required may differ from the number illustrated.

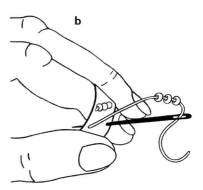

b. Working in the hand, ***straight-stitch*** the 3-bead sets diagonally along the ribbon. At the start and end of each set work ***knotting stitches*** on the back to maintain tension.

Thimble slippers – making up

These instructions apply to both thimble slipper projects. Each has five components: the Upper, the Sole, the lining for each, and a twisted cord for edging.

The stages of making up include:
• padding the boards for Upper and Sole
• mounting the embroidery
• lining and making up the Upper
• making and attaching the twisted cord
• mounting the silk on the padded Sole
• completing the slipper
A set of partly made up components is shown in Pl 19.

You will need:

Tools and materials. Sharp HB pencil, tracing paper; Dutch grey board* (445 gsm), scissors for cutting the board, adhesive (e.g. PVA glue), cotton buds, tweezers, paper towels for cleaning up; embroidery scissors, fine pins (silk pins)**, fine sewing needle.
Fabric. Small piece of extra heavy sew-in vilene or pellon to pad the upper and sole.
Threads. Viscose or silk sewing thread; teal green embroidery silk for twisted cord edging.

* found as backing on memo pads. ** dressmaker's pins are too thick!

Working notes

UPPER AND SOLE
Padding the boards. Always work on a clean surface.
1. Trace the solid outlines of the Upper and Sole, shown on your layout diagram, p.74. Turn over the tracing, pencil-side down, and re-trace on to the board.
2. Cut out the board shapes roughly with scissors, just outside the pencil outline. Next cut out the shapes accurately, using the middle of the blade.
3. *Upper.* Apply a thin layer of adhesive to one side of the board with a cotton bud. Place the board on the padding, adhesive side down, and let it set. Trim the padding to the board.

4. *Sole.* Repeat for the board of the sole and set aside. The padded side of the sole will be inside the slipper. *Don't* cut out any pattern parts yet.

Mounting the embroidery on the Upper
5. Centre the embroidery over the padded board and pin it in the order shown in Fig 1, see Pl 18. The method of pinning, from one side to the point directly opposite (on the straight grain), is important for an even finish. Turn over the panel and cut out the Upper.

Diagrams shown reduced

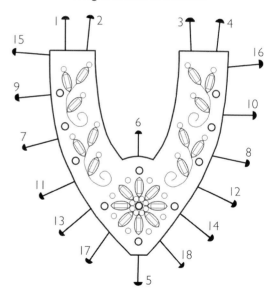

1. Pinning the embroidery to the board of the Upper

The embroidery is shown pinned to the padded board, as on Pl 18, and not cut out from the silk.

   Centre the embroidery over the padded board, and check by holding both up to the light. Start by pushing the pins into the straight edge of the board at *1, 2, 3 & 4.* At *5,* opposite, gently pull the fabric taut against pins *1-4* and insert pin *5.* Continue pinning in the order shown. Check the centering as you go and adjust the pins if necessary.

   Turn over the silk and cut round the tacked outline, which allows a 6 mm (¼ in) overlap, then cut out the inner section. Avoid dislodging the pins below.

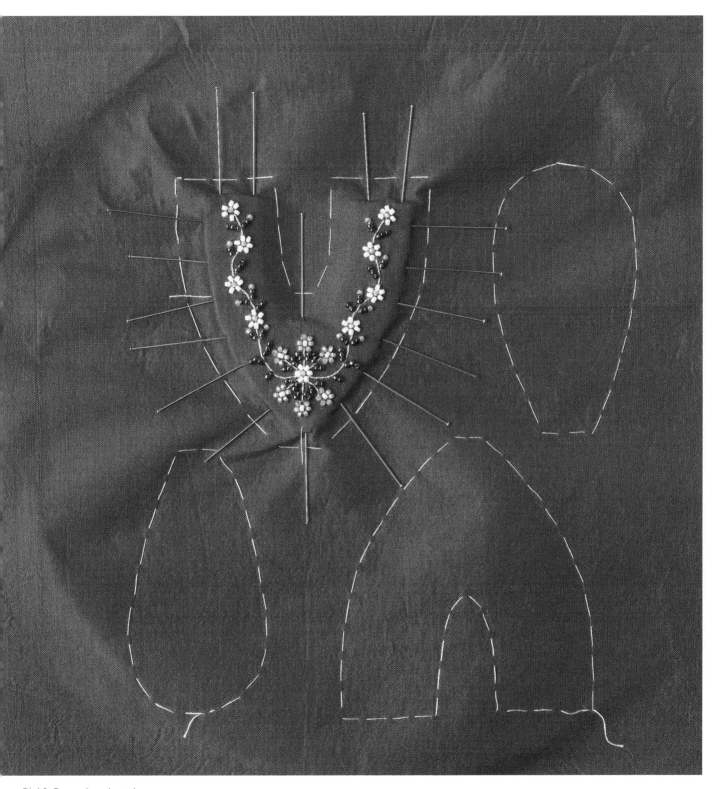

Pl 18. Pinned embroidery
The embroidery for the Upper is shown off the hoop and pinned to the padded board, as in Fig 1. Actual size.

6. Follow Fig 2 for cutting notches and gluing down the overlaps.

Lining the upper
7. Cut out the lining, leaving the inner edge uncut, Pl 19. Follow Fig 3 to pin the lining to the Upper.

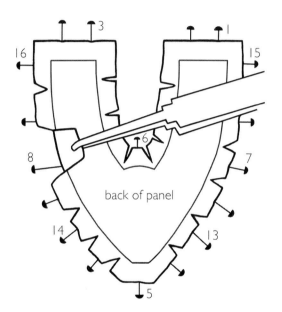 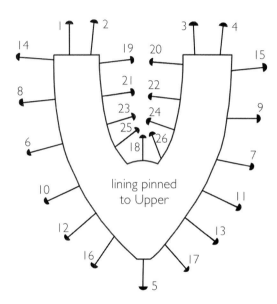

2. Gluing down the overlaps

Work with the back facing you. Cut notches (V-shaped or straight) *towards* the board edge, as shown, but *not* right up to it.

With a cotton bud, apply thin dabs of adhesive section by section, avoiding the corners. Glue down the overlap using tweezers. Start along an outer edge, pulling the fabric taut against the board edge and removing pins as you go, then the facing inner edge. Repeat for the other side. Press down and smooth out the fabric with the flat side of the tweezers.

Next glue the tip of the toe, followed by the inner curve opposite. Glue the top edges last. For the corners see *Needle book – making up*, Fig 3, p.98. Clean off any surplus glue with a paper towel.

3. Lining the Upper

This shows the lining pinned to the back of the Upper. When cutting out the lining, *don't* cut out the inner section (above the dotted line on the pattern layout) until you have pinned the outer edges, see Pl 19.

Cut out the lining, using the tacked outline on the fabric as a guide, which gives a 6 mm (¼ in) overlap. Cut notches round the curved outer edge: make them *slightly shorter* than those on the embroidered Upper (Fig 2).

Starting at the top, fold the overlap under and with wrong sides together align the fold along the top edge. Pin the fold into the edge of the embroidery in the order shown.

Continue round the outer edge, section by section, up to pin *17*. Adjust the pins if necessary so the lining is stretched evenly. Push the pin heads right in, **oversew** the outer edges, then remove the pins.

Now cut out the inner section. Cut the notches, carefully copying the angles shown in Fig 2 for the bottom corners. Pin the overlap in the order shown. Oversew the edges.

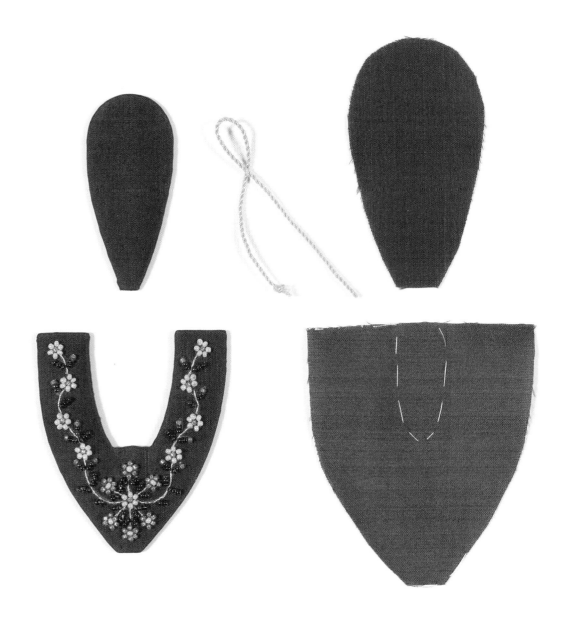

Pl 19. Thimble slipper Upper and Sole ready for lining
Clockwise, from bottom left. Embroidered Upper mounted on padded board; inner Sole mounted on padded board; twisted cord for edging; outer lining for Sole after cutting out; lining for Upper cut along the tacked outline, with the inner section uncut. The twisted cord was made from three strands of pink embroidery silk.

Shaping and making up the Upper
8. Follow Fig 4 to shape the Upper then oversew the back seam, which will later be covered by the twisted cord.

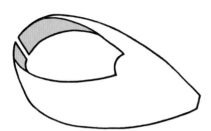

4. Shaping and making up the Upper
Place your thumbs on either side of the completed (flat) Upper with your index fingers beneath. Gently form the mounted board into the rounded slipper shape shown. Oversew the back seam.

Twisted cord

9. Use three strands of embroidery silk to make a **twisted cord** long enough to cover the top edge of the upper and the back seam. Follow Fig 5.

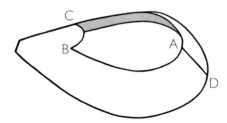

5. Securing the twisted cord to the Upper
Start at *A* with the looped end of the cord. Work *diagonal* stitches in matching viscose thread to couch the cord along the edge. The thread should lie hidden in the grooves of the cord. Couch in the order *ABCAD*.

About 6 mm (¼ in) beyond *D* bind the end of the cord with thread and cut off the rest. The bound edge will be tucked under the Sole outer lining later.

Mounting the silk on to the padded Sole
10. Centre the silk over the padded board. Pin the silk to the board following Fig 6.

Completing the slipper
11. With the padding inside the slipper, pin then oversew the sole edges to the completed Upper, Fig 7.
12. Pin and oversew the lining to the underside of the sole, Fig 8. Your slipper is now ready for its thimble!

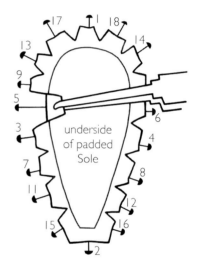

6. Mounting the silk on to the padded Sole
The Sole is shown with the underside towards you. Pin the silk to the board in the order shown.

Turn over the silk and cut round the tacked outline, which allows a 6 mm (¼ in) overlap. Avoid dislodging the pins.

Cut notches as shown and glue down the overlaps, following the general method of Fig 2, to complete the mounting.

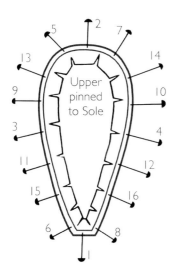

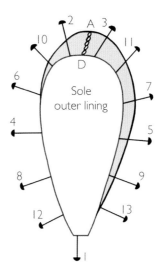

7. Joining the Sole to the Upper

The Sole is shown from beneath pinned to the Upper. Hold the Upper upside down and slot the Sole, board side facing you, just inside the Upper.

Hold the Sole and Upper in position and pin the edges together. Start with the tip of the toe and follow the order shown. *Oversew* the edges, working from toe to heel along each side. These stitches will later be covered by the outer lining.

8. Lining the underside of the Sole

The Sole is shown from beneath with lining pinned in position.

Cut out the lining pattern along the tacked outline on your silk, noting that the pattern is slightly larger than that for the inside Sole. With the silk side facing you, cut notches round the curved outer edge: make them *slightly shorter* than those on the inside Sole. Fold the overlaps under and pin the folds to the edge of the Upper in the order shown. Make sure the lining completely covers the *oversewing* and the end of the cord. Oversew the two edges and remove the pins.

Simple mounting – making up

This process applies to the Periwinkle and Greetings card projects.

The stages of making up are:
- cutting and padding a board
- mounting the embroidery on the padded board

You will need
Tools and materials. Metal ruler, craft knife with sharp blade, cutting surface or board, sharp HB pencil; mounting board (as for picture framing), adhesive (e.g. PVA glue), cotton buds, tweezers, paper towels for cleaning up; embroidery scissors, fine pins (silk pins)*.
Fabric. Polyester felt to pad the board.

* dressmaker's pins are too thick!

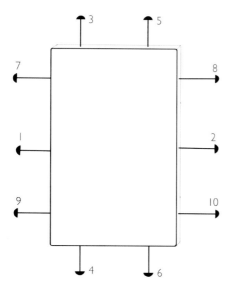

I. Pinning the embroidery to the padded board
Centre the embroidery over the padded board and pin it in the order shown.

Working notes
Padding the board with felt. Always work on a clean surface.
1. Measure the solid outline of the board on your layout diagram, p.68. Use the measurements to mark the outline on the mounting board and cut it out on a cutting board with a craft knife and metal ruler. Make sure the corners are right angles.
2. Use a cotton bud to apply a thin layer of adhesive to one surface. Place the board on the felt, adhesive side down, and let it set. Trim the felt to the board.

Mounting the embroidery on the padded board
3. Centre and pin the embroidery, Fig 1. Use *Needle books – making up* as a guide. The method of pinning, from one side to the point directly opposite (on the straight grain), is important for an even finish.
4. Check your embroidery is still centered and adjust the pins if necessary. Turn over the work and trim the surrounding fabric. Glue the edges and corners to the back of the board, Figs 2 and 3 on pp.97, 98. Remove the pins.
5. Cover the back of the panel by gluing a piece of plain paper to it.

Greetings card –
making up

The embroidery should already have been mounted on its padded board and a flat beaded edge added if desired.

The next stages of making up are:
- cutting and folding the backing card
- mounting the embroidered panel on the card

You will need

Card to suit the colour of your silk and embroidery; ruler, pencil, adhesive and craft scissors; a needle, and viscose or silk thread to match your fabric.

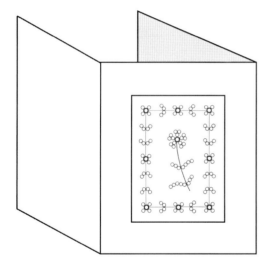

1. Preparing and assembling the greetings card

Cut a rectangle of card measuring 232 × 88 mm (9 × 3½ in) Divide the length into three and make two folds as shown. Make the left and middle folds 79 mm (3¹⁄₁₆ in) wide and the right (shaded) fold 74 mm (2⅞ in).

Position the embroidery on the centre panel as shown. Working from inside the card, stitch the edges to the card with one stitch per edge.

Apply adhesive round the edges of the right flap (shown shaded) and stick it to the back of the middle section, to hide the stitches.

The card can also be made larger to good effect. Figure reduced.

Glossary

Bodkin – Blunt ended needle with a long eye, used for threading ribbons, tapes and cords, mostly for *lingerie*.

Bugle beads – Tubular beads, see *Tools & materials*.

Cotton bud – A thin stick, tipped at both ends with cotton wool, available from pharmacies.

Dutch grey board – Light card, see *Tools & materials*.

Hoop frame – See Pl 7 and *Tools & materials*.

Metallic cord, **Metallic floss** – Synthetic threads, made in imitation of gold or silver, see *Tools & materials*.

Nymo thread – A strong nylon thread with flat section for threading beading needles.

Plunging – Taking a couched thread with the needle from the right side to the back of the fabric.

Purl – Metallic coiled 'thread', also known as 'gimp' or 'bullion', see *Tools & materials*.

PVA adhesive – A white, no run, glue, which dries clear and is water-soluble.

Seed beads – Bun-shaped beads, see *Tools & materials*.

Silk floss – Raw untwisted silk thread used in embroidery.

Twisted cord – A thin decorative rope, used here for edging or ties, made from strands of *coton perlé* or silk, twisted together to form a cord.

Whip stitch – A stitch designed to hold together threads of existing stitches, see Fig 4, p.86 and Fig 6, p.88.

Suppliers

BEADS, FABRICS, THREADS, BOOKS AND TOOLS
BY MAIL

Beads, tools & books
Carole Morris, Spangles, 1 Casburn Lane
Burwell, Cambridge CB5 0ED
Tel 01638 742024   www.spangles4beads.co.uk
Email spangles4beads@ntlworld.com

Beads including 3 mm bugles, tools & books
G J Beads, 1 & 3 Court Arcade, The Wharf
St Ives, Cornwall TR26 1LG
Tel 01736 793886   www.gjbeads.co.uk
Email beadyspice@aol.com

Beads, tools & books
The Spellbound Bead Co, 45 Tamworth Street
Lichfield, Staffordshire WS13 6JW
Tel 01543 417650   www.spellbound.co.uk
Email info@spellboundbead.co.uk

Beads including 3 mm bugles & books
The Bead Merchant, PO Box 5025
Coggeshall, Essex CO6 1HW
Tel 01376 563567   www.beadmerchant.co.uk
Email info@beadmerchant.co.uk

Beads
Charisma Beads, 25 Churchyard
Hitchin, Herts SG5 1HP
Tel 01462 454054   www.charismabeads.co.uk
Email vivien@charismabeads.co.uk

*Beads including petite, threads, vilene interfacing
& tools*
Stitches Needlecraft Centre, 355 Warwick Road
Solihull, West Midlands B91 1BQ
Tel 0121 706 1048   www.needle-craft.com
Email info@needle-craft.com

Silk fabric
Hilary Williams, The Silk Route, Cross Cottage
Cross Lane, Frimley Green, Surrey GU16 6LN
Tel 01252 835781   www.thesilkroute.co.uk
Email hilary@thesilkroute.co.uk

Silk embroidery threads
Pipers Silks, Chinnery's, Egremont Street
Glemsford, Suffolk CO10 7SA
Tel 01787 280920   www.pipers-silks.com
Email sales@pipers-silks.com

Polyester felt padding, appliqué needles, cutting mats
The Cotton Patch, 1285 Stratford Road
Hall Green, Birmingham B28 9AJ
Tel 0121 702 2840   www.cottonpatch.co.uk
Email mailorder@cottonpatch.net

*Opti-Visor binocular magnifier (various
magnifications). Best if you don't wear spectacles.*
Thomas Sutton Ltd
37/38 Frederick Street, Birmingham B1 3HN
www.suttontools.co.uk
Email info@suttontools.co.uk

Reproduction tools, including thimbles & scissors
Ray Coggle, James Swann and Son
PO Box 2797, Warwick CV34 4XR
www.jamesswann.fsbusiness.co.uk
Email ray@jamesswann.fsbusiness.co.uk